BRIGHT NOTES

THE EDUCATION OF HENRY ADAMS BY HENRY ADAMS

Intelligent Education

INFLUENCE PUBLISHERS

Nashville, Tennessee

BRIGHT NOTES: The Education of Henry Adams
www.BrightNotes.com

No part of this publication may be used or reproduced in any manner whatsoever without written permission, except in the case of brief quotations in critical articles and reviews. For permissions, contact Influence Publishers http://www.influencepublishers.com.

ISBN: 978-1-645424-18-5 (Paperback)
ISBN: 978-1-645424-19-2 (eBook)

Published in accordance with the U.S. Copyright Office Orphan Works and Mass Digitization report of the register of copyrights, June 2015.

Originally published by Monarch Press.
James R. Lindroth; Colette Lindroth, 1966
2019 Edition published by Influence Publishers.

Interior design by Lapiz Digital Services. Cover Design by Thinkpen Designs.

Printed in the United States of America.

Library of Congress Cataloging-in-Publication Data forthcoming.
Names: Intelligent Education
Title: BRIGHT NOTES: The Education of Henry Adams
Subject: STU004000 STUDY AIDS / Book Notes

CONTENTS

1)	Introduction to Henry Adams	1
2)	Introduction to The Education of Henry Adams	25
3)	Textual Analysis	
	Chapters 1–11	28
	Chapters 12–22	41
	Chapters 23–35	59
4)	Essay Questions and Answers	80
5)	Bibliography	84

INTRODUCTION TO HENRY ADAMS

HENRY ADAMS: 1838–1918

Birthplace

Henry Adams was born in Boston on February 16, 1838. Even at his birth the child seemed destined for greatness, at least as far as inheritance could provide greatness: his great-grandfather was John Adams, one of the writers of the Declaration of Independence and the second President of the United States, and his grandfather was John Quincy Adams, a brilliant statesman and sixth President of the country. If America had an aristocracy in the early nineteenth century, then surely the Adamses were a significant part of it; and if there was a cultural center in the nation, then that center was Boston. The family had a distinguished tradition of honorable, active service to their country, and all seven members of Henry's generation were expected to take their places in this tradition. The Adamses had wealth, power, ability and education, but not one of them would have considered using these assets for purely personal gain.

Quincy

Henry was a member of a large, closely knit family. Some of his earliest memories deal with his grandfather, John Quincy Adams, who lived in nearby Quincy and who was then serving as a member of Congress. Henry and his brothers and sisters spent many summers in the big family house at Quincy, and they became steeped in the atmosphere of politics which was so prevalent there. The table talk, which the children were allowed at times to partake in (and which they always listened to), often consisted of the conversations of prominent historians, orators, politicians and educators. Many of these prominent men became friends of young Henry as well as of his father, and correspondence with some of them, notably the orator Charles Sumner, continued well into Henry's young manhood. It was taken for granted that at least one of these young Adamses would serve his country in a high capacity; one of young Henry's vivid memories, in fact, is of an Irish gardener who remarked to him, "You'll be thinkin' you'll be President too!" This comment, which Adams includes in the *Education*, impressed the child strongly. He grew up trained in a tradition and expecting to serve this tradition. He was to contrast these easy assumptions of his youth with the doubts which assailed him later: "...no one suggested at that time a doubt whether a system of society which had lasted since Adam would outlast one Adams more." Of course this society did not "outlast one Adams more" - Henry - and this is the source of much of the stoical acceptance which one finds in the writings of Henry Adams.

Boston

If his father's family was singularly well versed in the arts of statesmanship, his mother, too, contributed a significant inheritance. When Henry was ten years old his grandfather Adams died; when he was eleven his mother's father, Peter Chardon Brooks, died and left what was popularly believed to be the largest estate in Boston to his children. After Henry's eleventh year the Adams family life centered more in Boston than in Quincy, for the Brooks family was very prominent there. The relationship between Henry and his Brooks cousins was close; without giving the matter any thought, the boy went to the "right" grammar school and the "right" church, and took his place in the most youthful segment of Boston society.

Schooling

One of the most important experiences of any young Bostonian was his schooling. Henry attended classes, of course, but his own testimony states that the most important part of his education was that which he acquired at home. Literary and political interests dominated the Adams family, and their father was fond of reading Longfellow, Tennyson, and other contemporary poets. Henry learned French, read eighteenth-century history, and in general acquired a fairly broad liberal education while still very young.

School's Restrictions

If Henry enjoyed his ability to select the finest writers and thinkers at home, however, he never felt the same fondness for school. "If school helped, it was only by reaction," he said in *the Education*. He explained that he disliked school so much that it became a positive, rather than a negative emotion. He disliked school because he was learning in a crowd rather than as an individual; he was forced to memorize things which seemed irrelevant to him; he was pressed into competing for prizes which he didn't want. Henry longed for time in which to grow at his own pace, developing with material of his own choice. Schoolmasters were constantly hurrying him, and forcing their own tastes on him.

What He Did Learn

Much as he hated school, he conceded that the experience gave him a usable acquaintance with mathematics and with languages, notably French, German and Spanish. Even so, he insisted that private study could have taught him more about these subjects than classroom work did. But these were the subjects which eventually proved useful to him.

Reading

If Henry's school experiences were unproductive, his independent reading was not. "Books were the...source of his life," and he read the major writers of his time - Thackeray, Dickens, Tennyson, Macaulay, Carlyle, Scott. He also partook in the social activities of the time, being especially fond of winter sports like sleighing and skating, but reading was the primary interest of his youth.

Harvard

For any intelligent and educated young man of Henry Adams' stature, the logical college had to be Harvard - and it was to Harvard College that Henry went in the fall of 1854. In his *Education* the Harvard years are called a waste of time, a "blank" period. This is usually considered an old man's recollection of the follies of youth, however, for evidence from his college years indicates that Henry must have enjoyed himself immensely. As usual, he was surrounded by the sons of famous men, and men who were to become famous in their own right. These friendships, apparently, were more of an education for him than his classes were.

Activities

Adams was a member and an officer of the Hasty Pudding Club, an undergraduate organization much interested in drama. Adams both wrote and acted in the plays which the club produced, and on several occasions gave orations for his fellow members. He also printed several articles in the *Harvard Magazine*, on books, politics and other topics of general student interest. In his senior year he won the Bowdoin Prize Competition for an essay. He was not an honor student, however; it seems apparent that his literary and social endeavors kept him from the highest honors in his classroom work. But his fellow students, if not his teachers, recognized his abilities, and he was chosen Class Orator for his senior year, an honor which he considered flattering and touching. He graduated in 1858, and if he considered Harvard a waste of time when he was an old man, apparently he did not while young; he commented, upon his graduation, that he "did not believe it would be possible to pass four pleasanter years."

Germany

After graduation from Harvard, Henry and a friend sailed for Germany, intending to study law in Berlin. He discovered that his knowledge of German was not up to the task, however, and instead of studying began to wander about as a tourist. He and his friends enjoyed the atmosphere, the beer, and the music, both classical and popular, which Germany offered; they took walking tours and tried to acquire some knowledge of the language. Eventually, however, Henry's sister convinced him that he was learning nothing practical in Germany, and he went to Italy with her for a few months.

Italy

The trip to Italy became Henry's first really practical writing experience, for he suddenly found himself a newspaper correspondent. The Italian rebel-patriot Garibaldi was coming to power just at that time, and Henry sent home records of the fighting which was going on. They were published in the Boston Courier and other papers in the area, and made some little reputation for their young author.

Home Again

Henry again answered the call of family, however. In 1860, though he was very much enjoying his stay in Europe, he came home to help serve his father, who was deeply involved in the turmoil of American Civil War politics. Eventually he went to England as an aide to his father, who was serving as Minister to the Court of Saint James, a position of great importance in those troubled times. These seven years which he spent in England were a revelation to the young man; his account of them is one of the most significant portions of the *Education*, and he himself called them the most important years of his life.

Literary Activity

Henry did not wish to discontinue his writing, even though he was deeply involved in political activities. He wrote anonymous comments on the goings-on in London, and sent them to the New York Times, whose editor received them gladly. This activity was ended, however, when the authorship was identified and Henry's activities were used in criticisms of his father. The writing stopped, then, except for official work, but Henry spent his spare time another way - he began extensive historical research, and later published several significant articles in the historical reviews. When he returned to America in 1868 he went to Washington, where he again took up journalistic activities. His first book, a collection of historical articles written by himself and his brother Charles, appeared in 1871; it was titled *Chapters of Erie and Other Essays*.

Back To Harvard

All of this writing had not gone unnoticed, either by the general public or by the scholars. Charles Eliot, then president of Harvard, was interested in the young Adams; after a considerable effort, he managed to persuade Adams to accept a job teaching history at Harvard. It was a position, then as now, which included a great deal of scholarly prestige, but Adams was not easily persuaded to accept it. He still disapproved of the teaching system, even as he had disliked it when a student, and he took the job on the condition that he might use some of his energies in a teaching reform, particularly in the teaching of history.

Teaching And Writing

If Adams intended to instill new life into the dusty business of teaching and studying history, he seems to have been more than successful. A significant number of his pupils eventually became historians of note, and they have been extravagant in their praise of Adams as a teacher and as an inspiration of their independent efforts. Along with his classroom work, however, Adams was still involved in writing. He was now editor of the *North American Review*, a magazine which assumed great prominence under his guidance. He printed articles by such literary men as Henry James and William Dean Howells, nearly doubled the circulation of the review, and increased its reputation both in scholarly circles and with the reading public. One of his students, Henry Cabot Lodge, was for a time co-editor with Adams, and eventually gained great prominence as a statesman and historian.

Marriage

But all was not scholarship and history with Adams. In 1872 he became engaged to Marian Hooper, a young Bostonian who had for some time been a friend of the family. They were married that year, and honeymooned in Europe. The marriage of Marian Hooper and Henry Adams has been considered unusually happy; both were intelligent, interesting, and much involved in the society of their fellows. Adams himself was lavish in his tributes to his wife, often asserting that whatever success he achieved in life was in large part due to her influence.

More Writing

The 1880's were years of great writing activity for Adams. He wrote his first novel, *Democracy, An American Novel*, in 1879, and it was published anonymously the next year. A biography, *John* Randolph, followed in 1882, and a pseudonymous novel, *Esther*, in 1884. During these years of creativity he was planning still another work, the massive and monumental *History of the United States of America During the Administration of Thomas Jefferson and James Madison*.

The History

This work has been considered one of the major contributions of nineteenth-century writing in America, and certainly holds first rank with histories of any nation. Adams chose the period, from 1801 until 1817, because he considered these years to be a significant unit in the history of the country. Jefferson ended the Revolutionary era, Adams felt, and had molded the future of the country in a manner which was to be felt for generations. *The History* includes all the characteristics which Adams' prose at its best exhibits - wit, **irony**, detachment, the feeling of complete objectivity. Completed in 1890, it will always be considered a significant milestone both in American literature and in history.

Travels Again

In 1886 Adams and a friend, the artist John LaFarge, had left for a tour of the South Seas and Japan. This experience, too, had literary significance for Adams, resulting in interesting memoirs and letters. In 1900 he visited the Paris **Exposition** and confronted the huge dynamo, whose silent power inspired what is perhaps the best-known section of *the Education*, "The Dynamo and the Virgin." The trip to Paris was also largely responsible for another of his most famous works, *Mont-Saint-Michel* and *Chartres*, published in 1904. This work, which Adams called "a study in thirteenth-century unity," is often considered a parallel piece to *The Education of Henry Adams*, which was published in 1907. In the *Education*, which he termed a "study of twentieth-century multiplicity," he takes up problems of the modern man, and predicts much of what the twentieth century has actually experienced - the loneliness, isolation and lack of values which has often been marked. *Chartres* is perhaps richer in feeling and color, less cynical and skeptical than the *Education*; both, however, are admirable documents of the thought of two vastly different eras.

The Death Of His Wife

If Adams' last works are colored by cynicism or near-despair, the fact can be in part accounted for by a personal tragedy which had occurred in 1885, the suicide of his wife. She had been the victim of states of depression for some time, and eventually took her own life. The tragedy of that fact is even deeper to the twentieth-century man, for Mrs. Adams' psychological problems were of a type which now could be lessened or even cured. In 1885 they could not, however, and Adams never entirely recovered from his wife's action. It sharply increased his aloofness, his pessimism; it might have at least been partially responsible for the unfavorable light in which he saw the twentieth century. The act also increased his literary output, however; the History and the following books were written at least in part in Adams' effort to take himself out of his own depression by submerging himself in scholarship and research.

Death

In 1912 Adams suffered a stroke, but recovered enough to continue to enjoy the family life which was still provided by young nephews, nieces and the rest of the numerous Adams family. Adams, who considered himself "an eighteenth-century man in the nineteenth century," actually lived until well into the twentieth century and modern history. He died on March 27, 1918, during the First World War. He had been highly regarded as a scholar and writer in his own time, but it was after his death that the real recognition of his talents came; he now ranks with the most significant and influential men of American letters.

INFLUENCES

His Environment

Boston, Quincy, and the inheritance of two family traditions exerted a strong and enduring influence on the character and writing of Henry Adams. He eventually rejected many of the ideals of the "Boston Brahmin" caste into which he was born, but he never forgot what had produced him, and he always looked upon himself as a product of his particular society. His upbringing would have been justifiably envied by most of the youths of his or any other time, yet as he grew older he declared that his training was outmoded, that the tradition which enshrouded him did not prepare him - for the twentieth century, or even for the nineteenth in which he lived most of his life. He always insisted that he was in fact an eighteenth-century man, trained in the tradition and integrity of an earlier day and not quite suited for his own. Whether or not this was true; whether Adams was, as he held, a man out of his time, or whether he was an admirable and sensitive recorder of the thoughts and attitudes of an era, the fact remains that he was an Adams of Boston, and these two things, family and home town, shaped his entire life.

Family History

The Adams family was in a very real sense an American dynasty, comparable to the great families who shaped the course of European history. Few other American families have combined longevity with such a history of service to the country; the elder John Adams' most famous contemporaries, George Washington, Benjamin Franklin and Thomas Jefferson, left no male descendants with the family name. This fact shaped Henry Adams' youth; the strict idealism of his father made him intensely aware of duty as a force; the wealth inherited by his mother gave him the leisure to perfect himself, to follow the intellectual and social pursuits at which he could excel.

Quincy

But there was a struggle even in this family inheritance, for the ties of Quincy, and the traditional Adams political stand, were opposed to those of Boston and his mother's family. Henry Adams always remembered the summers of his first ten years, spent at his grandfather Adams' residence; particularly he remembered the stern order of the household, and the fact that complete integrity was expected of everyone, from grandparents down to the youngest grandchildren.

Madam Adams

A shadowy but unforgettable figure in Adams' youth was "The Madam," his grandmother Adams. She was a European by birth, and Henry realized as a child that "she could never be Bostonian," but to the boy this was her chief charm. He recalled her as being "singularly peaceful, a vision of silver gray,...an exotic, like her Sevres china." It was his grandparents' influence, in large part, that made the child Henry at home in the eighteenth century. His grandmother especially he remembered as being, "like the furniture," a member of a more elegant and restrained society than either the nineteenth or the twentieth century were to be.

It was this European influence, Adams states in his memoirs, that may have made him not "of pure New England stock." It was not until 1845, he says, that "he quite accepted Boston, or Boston quite accepted him." Boston, at this time, was thoroughly steeped in colonialism, impressed by the majesty and correctness of English standards. The standards of Boston society before 1850 were the standards of England. Adams, the product of a more cosmopolitan culture, was never to be so impressed by authority as were his Boston contemporaries.

Religion

Another influence, or rather lack of influence, was seen by Adams in religion. His mother's family included some of the most prominent New England clergymen of the time, but Adams and his cousins "slept through their uncle's sermons, without once thinking to ask what the sermons were supposed to mean for them." The values of religion, Adams asserts in his *Education*, were replaced by the eighteenth-century values of his Grandfather Adams: "Resistance, Truth, Duty, Freedom."

Anchored in the standards of an earlier time, unprepared for what the twentieth century would bring, it is perhaps not surprising that Adams exhibited strong tendencies toward cynicism and pessimism in his last years.

Politics

It would be inconceivable that a child would not be shaped by the political career which Henry's father was pursuing, and by the companions which his parents entertained in the family house. Charles Francis Adams embraced the antislave cause, and this estranged him somewhat from the powerful Boston interests in 1848. "State Street," the symbol of Bostonian political power to Henry, was hostile to the elder Adams, and thus early in his life Henry became convinced that the practical route, the route of State Street and easy power, was not the best one. These issues were discussed often in the Adams home, and young Henry encountered the views of Ralph Waldo Emerson, Dr. Ellery Channing, Henry Wadsworth Longfellow and Oliver Wendell Holmes while still only a child. These views made a great impression on Henry, but the greatest single influence of his young life, and in a large part of his maturity, was still the steadfast integrity of his father.

Charles Francis Adams

Adams himself testifies to this influence in the first part of the *Education*: "His father's character was therefore the larger part of his education, as far as any single person affected it.... To his son Henry, the quality that distinguished his father was...that... he possessed the only perfectly balanced mind that had ever existed in the family." Henry pays tribute to his father's mental poise, his lack of self-consciousness or selfishness, his restraint and objectivity. These were qualities which the young man admired; they were also the qualities which he attempted to develop in himself; and they were, to a great extent, the qualities which exhibited themselves in his writing.

Standards And Stability

This devotion to duty and responsibility, his by right of birth and by long observation, was to remain with Henry for life. The men who surrounded his youth were statesmen rather than mere politicians; they were much more likely to guide public opinion than they were to be influenced by it. Thus the young Henry assumed a world of stability, the kind of world which existed in the Boston of the early nineteenth century. That the world would continue to rest on accepted standards was the assumption of most of Henry's contemporaries; as he himself said, "No one, except Karl Marx, foresaw radical change.... All experience...conspired to deceive and betray a twelve-year-old boy who took for granted that his ideas [and the ideas of his elders] would be respected." History, of course, was to prove the Adamses and their friends wrong. The world did not continue to accept the standards of the eighteenth and early nineteenth centuries, and it is not surprising that Henry Adams and others raised with these values should feel ill-prepared for the turmoil of the twentieth century.

Reading

But if the politicians and theologians of the nineteenth century failed to prepare Henry Adams for his time, there was one field in which he had the widest possible knowledge, and that was literature. The boy loved to read from the time of his earliest memory. He was not particularly fond of the stilted atmosphere of classroom and lessons, but on his own time he devoured all the books he could find. His father enjoyed reading aloud, and the Adams children listened to the speeches of Horace Mann, the poetry of James Russell Lowell, Henry Wadsworth Longfellow, and Alfred, Lord Tennyson. The elder Adams also exposed his children to the writing of Samuel Johnson and Alexander Pope, the prose and poetry masters of the eighteenth century. He was not fond of contemporary novelists, but Henry discovered them by himself, and read all the Dickens, Thackeray and Scott that he could find. He also immersed himself in the histories of Macaulay and Carlyle, which in many respects influenced his own approach to the study and writing of history.

Schools

However much Adams hated grammar school, it had an obvious and undeniable effect on him - if only because it made him resolve to modernize teaching procedures if he ever got the chance. But beyond that resolution, which he put into practice while he taught at Harvard, Adams' school years were productive in friendships and social activities if not in acquired knowledge. Adams, who even during his college years still felt himself not really a proper Bostonian, numbered among his friends a group of "outsiders," young men who were not from the New England area. One of these outsiders was "Roony" Lee, the son of Robert E. Lee of Virginia, one of the Confederacy's most famous generals during the Civil War. Other friends were Oliver Wendell Holmes, Jr., William Endicott and Henry Hobson Richardson, destined to be one of his century's greatest architects.

Writing And Drama

Adams is harsh in his treatment of a Harvard curriculum in his *Education*; he asserts that he never heard the names of Karl Marx or Auguste Comte, "the two writers of his time who most influenced its thought." But, if he did not profit much from his classes, he did from his spare time - he wrote, as much and as extensively as he could. As usual, his own opinion of his writing was harsh; he judged his writing as being without "wit or scope or force." But the effort was invaluable in view of his later career, for it gave him a period of comparative leisure in which he could experiment with many forms, try to find his limits, without being publicly embarrassed or being pressed by deadlines. The Harvard years were fertile ground for his writing abilities, if not for his education, for it was here that he conceived the idea which was later materialized as the *History*.

London

The early experience which Adams himself considered most influential was his stay in London with his father. The job of aide to the Minister to the Court of St. James gave the young Adams a unique opportunity to view the world of politics and society firsthand. It made him a wiser, if somewhat sadder, young man; when the seven years were up and he was returning to America, Adams felt that he had learned much about the dependability and honesty of the average man. Again, this experience had a direct influence on his later writings; it is hardly surprising that a young man from such an idealistic and duty-conscious background, thrown into all the sophistication and intrigue of European politics, should emerge considerably disillusioned and considerably more skeptical than he had been before. The cool realism with which he viewed London politics often appears as skeptical pessimism by the time the *Education* was written; the **irony** and detachment were never lost, however.

The Death Of His Wife

If Boston, his family, his friends and his education exerted good influences on Adams, the tragic death of his wife was felt just as powerfully. Adams' biographers have generally agreed that he was unusually fond of the companionship of women - at that time, most men thought rather slightingly of women's intellectual prowess, but Adams was very much an exception. He considered that women exerted a peculiar religious force in nature (an idea he was to investigate in "The Dynamo and the Virgin"), and he needed that quality in his life. His wife had filled the need, admirably, and he was violently upset at her death. He refused all companionship for a time, and it was only very gradually that he began going back into society. He saw his own family first, then close friends, and eventually the public again - but he never was quite the same man after his wife's death that he had been before it. He never mentioned her name; he turned increasingly from the present into the past. This accounts for much of what has been called pessimism in his later books, but there is another source for that emotion; what the world considered pessimism was, in many cases, simply the ironic pose which Adams took in order to hide the depth of his true feeling.

Renewed Activity

There was, however, one constructive activity to which Adams could turn after his bereavement: his writing. He threw himself into his work with more than his usual energy, in an attempt to remove himself from personal tragedy. He completed a volume of his *History* for publication, then left for an Eastern tour with his artist friend, LaFarge. He returned from this with a more relaxed attitude, and began working unreservedly on the History; he finished it, as he told his friends, in part as a monument to his wife.

The fact that Adams never wrote another history after this first massive attempt is usually accounted for by his wife's death. There is evidence from his correspondence that he could not undertake another labor so gigantic without her support and encouragement; he didn't care to please the professional historians, and the personal inspiration which his wife had supplied simply could not come from another source. At any rate, he turned to new literary pursuits after the death of his wife and the completion of the *History*.

The South Seas

Adams had found little respite on his trip to Japan, but another Oriental tour, this time to Tahiti and the other Pacific islands, was more rewarding. He was much impressed by what he called the "literary and artistic" conception of life in Tahiti, and printed a small volume of memoirs of Mauau Taaroa, the Last Queen of Tahiti. Another, less predictable sideline was also begun on the Tahitian trip. Adams took up painting, under the coaching of his friend LaFarge. He never showed great talent, considering himself too tightly disciplined to be a real artist, but he immensely enjoyed the experience. If Adams did not become a startlingly original painter, however, the experience did have one far-reaching effect: it was his painting in the South Seas that interested Adams more in European art, and was indirectly responsible for *Mont-Saint-Michel* and *Chartres*. The amazing sensitivity to color and line which is present in that book was the result of his artistic hobby. As proof of this, Adams sent LaFarge a copy of the book, with the inscription "from his pupil, H. A."

Europe

Adams traveled to Europe as a youth and as a mature man, and these experiences were probably the ones which most directly influenced his life and his philosophy, aside from his family and his relationship with his wife. It was the trip to the Paris **Exposition** of 1900 that seemed to put Adams face to face with the twentieth century, and it was this confrontation which resulted in what is now probably his most-read book, *The Education of Henry Adams*. Surrounded by the antiquity of the Gothic cathedrals of France, Adams was all the more appalled by the silent, efficient super-power of the dynamos at the **Exposition**; his assessment of these dynamos as the guiding force of the twentieth century has since been accepted as a startlingly accurate prediction.

SUMMARY

Adams, then, was the product of many different forces: his surroundings, his family, his friends, his travels. He was also, of course, uniquely individual, and it is this individuality which makes his writing so readable 'even today. When reading the *Education* one is not primarily aware of Henry Adams, the proper Boston Brahmin, Harvard - trained and contributing to the respectable literary and historical reviews. One is instead very much aware of the cool, ironic, detached observer of society, the man who caught with great accuracy the spirit of his own time and predicted much of what would happen in the time after he had died.

GENERAL SCHEME

Reputation With His Contemporaries

During his lifetime, Henry Adams was considered primarily an educator and historian, not a literary man. Both his novels, *Democracy* and *Esther*, were printed without his name, the first anonymously and the second under a pseudonym. The second, in fact, was positively submerged by its author, for he refused to have it advertised, and so greatly limited its sale. He was well known in social and political circles of his day, and was acquainted with many literary figures, but was not really one himself. He rejected, in fact, the often tedious and unrewarding job of trying to compete with other writers for place in the journals of his day. He was too much of an individualist, too reluctant to "go down into the rough-and-tumble" to work at making a literary name for himself.

Reputation Today

Ironically enough, it is in the mid-twentieth century that his literary reputation has become established. *The Education of Henry Adams*, posthumously published in 1919, was largely responsible for this late prominence. Coming as it did to a generation of jaded, war-sated intellectuals, the *Education*, with its weariness, cynicism and stoicism, seemed the appropriate statement for the times. The post-World War I generation was itself thoroughly disillusioned, and they responded to the book's cool assessment of a society without values. The next generation, which had World War II to contend with, responded with equal enthusiasm to Adams' prediction of an unprincipled "Atom King," a force without soul or principle, but only with power. And today's society, which in large part feels itself ruled by that very "Atom King" that Adams foresaw, is often inclined to view him as a prophet of sorts. It would seem that, ironically, Adams is a man out of his time just as he said he was; rather than being the eighteenth-century man he thought he was, however, he seems to have been a twentieth-century man unawares. Whatever the reason, Adams' literary stature has grown vastly since his death. This has happened, of course, with several of his contemporaries. The post-World War I society rejected the sentimental optimism of such former greats as Henry Wadsworth Longfellow, and the nineteenth-century reputations which have survived this re-evaluation are the searchers and the seekers, like Herman Melville and Nathaniel Hawthorne, or the cynics and the realists, like Mark Twain, Henry James, and William Dean Howells.

The Biographies

It is not just an accident that Adams' literary reputation is now secure, however. He was always a versatile writer, trying himself in such varied forms as the drama, the novel, biography and history. His two most important biographies were highly regarded when they were written, and are still considered masterpieces of the form. *Albert Gallatin* is a study of Jefferson's Secretary of the Treasury, notable for the precision of its documentation and the sureness of characterization. *John Randolph* is the study of an arrogant, talented man who abused his gifts. The two books, taken together, reveal as much about their author as they did about the figures they were concerned with. They, like the *Education*, are studies in human capacities and the human personality.

The History

The gigantic *History of the United States of America During the Administration of Thomas Jefferson and James Madison* has always ranked as a literary and historical landmark in America. The book gives, not only an accurate historical and factual account of the years involved, but a vivid sense of the times, of the ideas which were shaping the country then and which would be influential far into the future. *The History* is memorable for still another fact, however; in it Adams gives an account of his own theory of history, his concern about the force which shaped a nation and carried it along. This force, viewed in another light, was to be the subject of his *Education* and of *Mont-Saint-Michel* and *Chartres*.

The Education Of Henry Adams

This book, which is now the most widely read of Adams' works, has been called "quite simply the greatest autobiography of American letters," and yet it is not strictly an autobiography at all. It is a wryly humorous account of the "education" of an idealistic young man, an education which did not really begin until he realized that he knew nothing at all. It is an interesting study in objectivity, for, though Adams does not mention some facts of his life, those which are pertinent to his "education" process are told with complete detachment. Rather than being simply an account of his own life, it is a universalized study of a young man confronted by a career, a young man who will have to contend with all of life, most of the time not understanding what he is involved in. Adams himself concludes with stoicism in the book; the reader, however, is not forced to accept his conclusion, but is perfectly free to adopt some other conclusion of his own.

Mont-Saint-Michel And Chartres

This book, written only four years before the *Education*, might have been written by another man. The love of painting, of color and design, which Adams acquired in his travels with LaFarge shine through here, illuminating Adams' love of the beauty which he encountered in the old Gothic cathedrals. But this is more than an artist's appreciation of interesting architecture; it is even more than history. It is in a very real sense a contact with the past itself, with the very essence of the Middle Ages. So steeped was Adams in the feeling of the thirteenth century that he seems almost able to conjure up that immediacy for the reader of the book; it is, for reader as well as for author, very much a "study in thirteenth century unity."

Versatility

Obviously, then, Adams was a most versatile writer. It was his talent to make history come alive, to people the past with characters who were at once true to life and revealing of the future. He worked equally well in the medium of personal memoir, factual history, biography and the novel. It is not surprising, then, that he should be taking his place with the great literary men of his century.

THE EDUCATION OF HENRY ADAMS

INTRODUCTION

THE PLAN OF THE BOOK

The Education is organized chronologically, beginning with the birth of the author and extending to his seventieth year. The experiences of the young Adams are at first grouped according to places (for example "Quincy," "Boston," "Washington," the towns in which he spent most of his youth). Later groupings are made around situations ("The Battle of the Rams," for example), or, more commonly, ideas or concepts which then involved the man: "Dilettantism," "Chaos," "Failure." Thus it seems obvious that Adams arranged the significant events of his life around those places, persons or attitudes which, at one time or another, most deeply involved him.

POINT OF VIEW

One of the most interesting and important considerations of the *Education* is its strange point of view: it is an autobiography told, not in the predictable first-person "I," but in the third person. Thus, Adams consistently refers to himself in the book, not as "me" or "I," but as "Adams," "the young man," "the private secretary" or "he." This of course seems strange at first; if someone is writing about himself, as Adams avowedly is, the reader expects the man to refer to himself personally. The technique, however, has many advantages as Adams uses it. For one thing, it removes the possibility of the book's being too personal; memoirs can be positively painful if the man is revealing unpleasant or embarrassing things about himself. Second, the use of the third person keeps the book from becoming tedious. One of the commonest drawbacks of autobiographies is that the reader may become bored with the "I" after four or five hundred pages. Third, the technique helps Adams to retain his air of detachment, of removal, of ironic objectivity, towards himself and his material. Fourth, the use of the third person keeps at a minimum the possibility of bitterness or didacticism (preachiness); since Adams is apparently writing about someone other than himself it is quite possible for him to comment objectively and coolly on whatever is going on. Fifth, the use of the third person is largely responsible for the humorous quality of the book. Since the reader is always aware that he is reading Adams' comments on Adams, the wit and wry amusement is always evident. And last, it is this objectivity and humor which enables the reader to take Adams' comments on himself as general statement relevant to much of society, rather than just as personal comments relevant only to himself.

INTENT

Adams states in his Preface that he has very definite reasons for writing the *Education*. He first quotes Jean Jacques Rousseau, who asserts in his Confessions that he wishes to unveil himself, in all his ugliness and folly, his goodness and sublimity - in other words, to give a full picture of himself. Adams goes on to say that this intention, fine for Rousseau, will not do for him; he intends this *Education* to serve as a model for self-teaching. He will, then, rather than reveal the Ego, discuss the "garment" which the young man should wear; he will attempt to reveal the extent to which society fits a young man for getting along in society.

> **Comment: Thus it is clear at the outset that the *Education* is to be taken as a social document. Adams is not attempting to reveal himself as a man, stripped naked before God and his fellow man. He is, instead, trying to consider his own position in the modern world, and the extent to which his upbringing and education fitted him for the world in which he had to live. He will also be redefining the word "education" itself; he makes it clear in his Preface that the actual process of education has nothing to do with so limited an experience as schooling, but in fact is the entire process of life itself.**

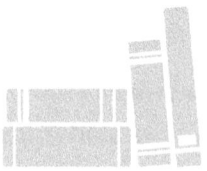

THE EDUCATION OF HENRY ADAMS

TEXTUAL ANALYSIS

CHAPTERS 1-11

CHAPTER I: QUINCY

In the first chapter Adams takes up his birth in Boston, and considers the fact that he was "branded" by his background and location, destined at birth for a certain kind of career. He considers both the good and bad possible effects of being born an Adams in Boston. On one hand, he will not be free to decide what path he wishes to follow, but on the other hand, he was born possessing advantages which many men never achieve after a lifetime.

The Weight Of Tradition: Adams also comments in the first chapter of the immense weight of tradition which bore on "ten pounds of unconscious babyhood," and questions whether that baby will ever know such a thing as liberty or choice. This will be one of the questions which Adams considers at most length during the book: can man choose to do what he wishes, or is he in a large part determined by his inheritance and environment? The question is never fully answered, of course, since Adams himself never reached a satisfactory conclusion. It is considered at length, however, in the book.

The remainder of Chapter I is a recollection of a boy's experience in his grandparents' home, and the distinct effect which Adams felt, even as a ten-year-old, witnessing the funeral of the man who had been both his grandfather and the sixth President of the United States.

CHAPTER II: BOSTON

Adams goes on to consider himself as a growing boy attending grammar school and becoming familiar with many of the overwhelming political and moral questions of the day. He again takes up the problem of inheritance, in this case the considerable wealth which his family inherited from his maternal grandfather. The two central problems which he considers in this chapter are the moral choices which he felt confronting his father (and thus himself) and the lack of valuable experience or information to be acquired at school. The problems of school and moral choice are connected, for Adams makes it clear that the only place a young man of his age could obtain moral standards was at home; Adams himself acquired these standards most of all from his father.

Adams' Description Of His Father: It is the character of his father, Charles Francis Adams, which most stands out in this chapter. Henry Adams pays his father a magnificent tribute here, considering him as the "only perfectly balanced mind" that the family had possessed, and possibly the only one that he ever knew. It was his father's standard of Duty, Truth, Freedom and Resistance that the child adopted; it was these standards, he indicates, that shaped his life and perhaps made him unable to cope with the twentieth century.

CHAPTER III: WASHINGTON

This chapter contains one of the first really amusing incidents in the book, an incident which gives evidence that, though an Adams, Henry was also very much a real little boy. It is a long description of a series of winter fights between the "proper" Boston boys and the toughs, a fight which was almost invariably won by the toughs because of superior numbers and unseemly tactics. Violence, then, was a part of education, even for a Boston boy of good family.

Slavery: The remainder of the chapter deals with Henry's journey to Washington with his father, and his first exposure to the national political scene. His comments on the Senate are again amusing; his comments on seeing slavery firsthand are revealing of his sense of decency. Slavery was a nightmare to the boy, the essence of wickedness and depravity. At first Adams longed, like the slaves, to escape back to "free territory"; as he remained longer in the South, however, he began to realize that the issue of slavery, like everything else, was many-sided. He eventually felt drawn to the heavy, indolent atmosphere of the South; his Puritanical, Boston soul felt tempted by the formlessness, the indolence, the "swagger" he felt in the South. Even at twelve, young Adams realized that Boston and Washington were not two different worlds, but simply revealed two different aspects of man; at the time, he was not sure which he might choose, if pressed.

Free Choice: At the end of Chapter Three, Adams again confronts the problem of free choice. He felt, he states, that he was unprepared and unable to make moral decisions like choosing between the issues of slavery or Free Soil. "He should have been, like his grandfather, a protege of George Washington, a statesman designated by destiny, with nothing to do but look directly ahead, follow orders, and march." This is one of the major distinctions which Adams will draw between the eighteenth and the twentieth centuries: in past times, men could see visible symbols of authority and put their faith in these symbols. Twentieth-century man, however, has lost the symbols (church hierarchy, kings, uniforms) and so every man is faced with the problem of choice and decision throughout his life.

> **Comment: In the first three chapters, Adams introduces one of his major topics, the problem of choice which faces modern man. He gives an accounting of his parental background and his youthful environment, and indicates the effects which these influences had on his life. He concludes Chapter Three with a comment on the change which lay before the world: the American boy in 1854 stood "nearer the year 1 than to the year 1900." Tradition did not equip the nineteenth-century boy for the scientific and moral revolution of the twentieth century; man was faced with the unceasing problem of choice, and he had nothing left to help him guide his choice. This was Adams' problem, and, by implication, it is the problem of Western man.**

CHAPTER IV: HARVARD COLLEGE

This chapter is more light-hearted in tone than was the previous one. It is an account of his college years, and he considers the motives which sent his contemporaries to Harvard (custom, social ties, convenience) and the comparative lack of character which the Harvard education imparted. Harvard, Adams says, probably didn't do much harm to its students - it didn't teach much, but then it didn't impart many prejudices, either. At least the Harvard graduate was comparatively unbiased, he added; if he was not educated, then at least he remained ready to receive knowledge when the occasion would present itself.

His Schoolmates: Adams also considers many of his college friends in this chapter, and though he states that they learned nothing from each other, this is probably to be considered an exaggeration. If Adams and his friends were naive and sometimes foolish, as he says, then so are most other young men of college age. What is evident from this chapter is the strong bond of friendship which united Adams and his colleagues; the section on Harvard reveals that whether or not he received an education there, he enjoyed himself, and was pleased by the student honors which he received.

Writing: Adams also considers the beginnings of his writing career in this chapter, and though, characteristically, he is highly critical of his early work, it is again evident that this apprenticeship was beneficial to him. He worked at his writing as hard as he could and most of his ambitions were rewarded when he was named Class Orator by his classmates. Adams says "he never understood how he managed to defeat not only a more capable but a more popular rival," but again it is quite clear that the young man was pleased by the honor.

Comment: The section on Harvard ends with Adams' reaffirmation that, neither as boy nor man, had he any faith in formal schooling. He comments on the lack of individuality which can be detected among college men, concluding that this is perhaps the result of a lack of individuality on the part of the

college itself. This is another of the themes which he will deal with repeatedly in the *Education:* the problem of remaining an individual when one is a part of a mass society. Adams concludes this chapter with his statement that "as yet he knew nothing. *Education* had not begun."

CHAPTER V: BERLIN

After Adams graduated from Harvard he went to Germany with a friend, and this chapter takes up his experiences abroad. Again, it is amusing; his first experience with seasickness, he says, taught him more than all his formal schooling. It taught him that there is such a thing as misery which must be endured. Adams is again humorous in his treatment of the brash young American (himself) who elects to study law in German and Latin, only to discover that he actually knows very little about either language. But if American students are laughable, so are German professors, and Adams is at his best in describing the system of German education which, as he says, is founded on the "lecture system in its deadliest form as it flourished in the thirteenth century."

Beethoven: Adams decided, then, that "neither the method nor the matter nor the manner" of German legal education could profit him, and so he decided to seek his education for a time in life rather than in textbooks. He was unimpressed by German society, though he spent some time in the beer halls, eating sauerkraut and sausages with his friends; the famous German music meant nothing to him until he found himself enjoying the orderly structure of a Beethoven piece. He was astonished at himself, having thought that he was insensible to music; eventually he discovered that music, and particularly

Beethoven, was a "new sense" which "burst out like a flower into his life."

If his sense of music awoke in Germany, however, his sense of color and form did not, nor did his sense of metaphysics. Adams asserts that he was untouched by German thought generally, remaining insensitive to their philosophic and literary idols, Hegel, Kant, Goethe and Schiller. Eventually, he says, he discovered that he wasn't enjoying Berlin at all, and resolved to leave the place at once.

CHAPTER VI: DISPUTE

Adams and his friends toured the rest of Germany for a time after leaving Berlin. Adams was interested in Germany then, finding the country "medieval" in its politics, its society and its religion. Suddenly he found himself face to face with a moral problem; France and Germany were disputing each other's territorial gains, and Adams was forced to evaluate for himself the claims of the two countries. Adams is ironic in his assessment of himself as a moralistic American trying to find moral foundations for the political machinations of sophisticated Europe - but at least his education was continuing, for he was seeing history in action rather than on the pages of his textbooks.

Italy: Adams' moral quandary over the French-German problem came to a sudden end when his sister settled things for him. She decided that he was becoming Germanized, and since she disliked Germany she solved the problem by demanding that he accompany her to Italy. Adams' contact with his sister here is interesting, for it is at this point that he introduces another of his major ideas: that women, with their "positive moral sense" and their tendency to decide questions instinctively, are actually superior over men in many instances. As he states it: "It was his first experiment in giving the reins to a woman, and he was so much pleased with the results that he never wanted to take them back again. In afterlife he made a general law of experience - no woman had ever driven him wrong; no man had ever driven him right."

Comment: This statement on his sister in particular and women in general is interesting, since it shows the contrasting forces which he later develops at length in "The Dynamo and the Virgin." Women, to Adams, represent a positive spiritual force, unifying in its effect. Women, who act instinctively, are considered by Adams to be a synthesizing or unifying force. Men, who insist on acting on their reason, are generally divisive. The Virgin, the woman-symbol, stands for unity, stability and order, to Adams. The dynamo, the product of man's mind, stands for just the opposite - division, disorder and the lack of foundation.

Italy: Italy proved to be a largely happy experience for Adams. It "passed Beethoven as a piece of education." Adams compares Italy to music; rather than being a means to an end in education, it is in itself an end, in its richness of color, its diverse geography, its varied peoples. Adams asserts that he never cared for "landscape education" after Italy, since he was so impressed with that first experience. Italy, then, was an education in itself.

Garibaldi: Speaking practically, Italy also provided another kind of education. Adams became a correspondent for the *Boston Courier*, sending reports of the rebellion being led by Garibaldi, the Italian rebel-patriot. The young man was granted a personal interview with Garibaldi, and was much impressed by the color and noise of him and his "pirate staff." As usual, Italy was linked with music in Adams' mind; he compares the rebel camp to an opera by Rossini.

> **Comment: Adams, the intellectual and well-bred Bostonian, was much impressed with the force and vigor of Garibaldi. He later considered the man and his movement as a symbol of what eventually happened to the world: in his view, "society was dividing between the banker and the anarchist." But whether or not Garibaldi was a force for good, Adams could not fail to be impressed by his ability to act; as he says, the man's "energy was beyond doubt," even if his values perhaps were not.**

CHAPTER VII: TREASON

This chapter deals with Adams' return from Europe, his half-guilty acknowledgment that, in his father's eyes at least, he might have been wasting his time in Europe. From Adams' own point of view, of course, these months of activity and worldly experience were more of an education than all of his years of school; be that as it may, however, he willingly agreed to go to Washington to help his father with his official burdens. Washington was in turmoil, since Secession was in the air and the Civil War was only months away. Adams' comments on these scenes of confusion are a brief history in themselves. Among other things, the chapter includes illuminating personal comments on some of the major political powers of the time: Sumner and Seward, and of course Lincoln himself. The chapter is a study in power politics, dealing as it does with the struggles of these men; it is also ironic, however, since it closes with

Adams himself, still the untried young man returning docilely to Boston with his family.

New Experiences: Adams' education was taking a step forward at this time, however, as he himself acknowledges. As his father's private secretary, he could observe much of what was going on, and could form conclusions as to the standards of the men who were then shaping the future of the United States. It is customary for the modern American to regard the first months of Lincoln's administration as a time of exceptional political activity; Adams' characteristically wry comment on the time, however, is: "All that Henry Adams ever saw in man was a reflection of his own ignorance, and he never saw quite so much of it as in the winter of 1860–61." By now the reader is becoming accustomed to Adams' clear-eyed **realism** when evaluating statesmen and state moves. The politicians of Washington were not, perhaps, so different from Garibaldi and his "pirate staff" - except that the latter were more colorful.

CHAPTER VIII: DIPLOMACY

This chapter is one of the more personal statements in the book. It deals with the position of young Henry Adams watching his contemporaries (even his brother Charles) going off to war, but not going off to war himself. The young man felt the inappropriateness of his action; he was going to a secure and interesting position helping his father in England, while his friends and relatives were engaged in fighting. As Adams says, "Few things were for the moment so trivial in importance as the solitary private secretary crawling down to the wretched... steamer...to start again for Liverpool." Typically, Adams does not criticize those who were responsible for his position, but simply comments on it; the contrast between the fighters in America and the diplomats in London, however, underlies the entire chapter and makes it pointedly satiric. His comment at the end of the chapter is revealing of his whole attitude toward diplomacy: "Whatever might be the advantages of social relations to his father and mother, to him the whole business of diplomacy and society was futile."

> **Comment: Another of Adams' major ideas, less obviously stated than some of his others, is evident in this chapter as it was in the previous one. Adams constantly contrasts the man of action with the man of indecision, the man who lives physically with the man who lives primarily intellectually. This seems to be one of his chief points on the subject of "good family": the man who is too much the intellectual, too much the Boston Brahmin, can find himself paralyzed and unable to act.**

CHAPTER IX: FOES OR FRIENDS

The beginning of this chapter contains Adams' direct comment on war. It was not the war which especially shocked him, he says; it was rather the "ferocious joy of destruction" which appalled him, as well as the misdirection of this destruction. Adams had been college friends with many Southerners, and he could not think without pain of those friends being killed. If anyone was to be killed, he adds with ironic venom, it should be the British and American diplomats. This entire chapter is an ironic parallel between two kinds of death: the sudden and violent death of war, and the insidious, slow harrying-to-death which could result from too much "diplomacy." The chapter is also an investigation of morality, for Adams still felt that he should perhaps enlist and fight. His responsibilities to his father and his post, however, prevented this. Thus in the end he was left behind a desk, doing the job which looked easy but was really difficult, held there because of the stern tradition to duty in which he had been raised.

Literary Interests: The chapter is appropriately titled, however, for if it deals with the foes of war, it also deals with Adams' own friends - in this case, the authors whom he was discovering and trying to imitate. Adams mentions especially Victor Hugo, an old idol of his, and Algernon Charles Swinburne, then a new poet and a man whom Adams envied for his lyric ability. As usual, Adams is unsparing of his own talents in relation to people like Swinburne, Walter Savage Landor, and others; but the chapter is interesting in its revelation of Adams' sound literary judgments.

CHAPTER X: POLITICAL MORALITY

The reader who has already become familiar with Adams' attitudes will not be surprised to discover that "Political Morality" is an ironic chapter. Like other parts of this section of the *Education*, this is an interesting study of the devious methods of power politics. The junior secretary (Adams himself) was in an excellent position to judge the morality, or lack of it, of the statesmen he observed, and as he says, "...the position was irregular...yet it lent itself to a sort of irregular education that seemed to be the only sort of education the young, man was ever to get." Adams himself was in no position to influence any of the important activities around him, since he functioned mainly as a clerk. He could watch, however, and watch he did, till he reached the conclusion that, when reputations were at stake, the highest ministers of state were no more to be trusted than was the paper-seller on the corner.

Comment: Adams was quite sincere in his evaluation of his English years as an education. They were an education in cynicism, a realization that honor or villainy can be found in anyone, that politics is a rough business, that the individual would always to some extent be a victim of the mass. This lack of individuality had been felt by Adams in his years at Harvard; as he grew older, the idea was to become more and more powerful, and more and more disturbing to him.

CHAPTER XI: THE BATTLE OF THE RAMS

This chapter continues Adams' ironic commentary on the state of political morality, or lack of it. Here Adams considers the growth of real power in Washington, contrasting the new firmness to the state of indecision and vacillation which had existed there. The campaign of 1863, which was one of the decisive years of the Civil War, was making itself felt in Europe; "The private secretary" (Adams) watched with awe as a series of massive blows fell. As usual, Adams was fascinated by this study in power - "in that form, education reached its limits." As usual, Adams was simply observing the situation, rather than taking active part in it; and, as usual, he comments ironically on the fact in his writing. Again, his wry commentaries on the foibles of such political notables as Earl Russell and Gladstone are amusing and realistic; one would be unlikely to overestimate political minds after reading the *Education*. Certainly, Adams did not overestimate these minds after his contacts with them.

THE EDUCATION OF HENRY ADAMS

TEXTUAL ANALYSIS

CHAPTERS 12-22

CHAPTER XII: ECCENTRICITY

This chapter of the *Education* is especially interesting for the student of literature, since Adams here evaluates political types through the use of literary comparisons. He mentions especially William Makepeace Thackeray and Charles Dickens, English novelists who were famous for their satiric portraits of typical Englishmen. Adams insists that Thackeray was not exaggerating at all, and he quotes Thackeray's own words to the effect that he had simply described people as they were. Adams admits that Dickens did exaggerate, but again he concludes that the exaggeration was minor. The implication is, of course, that the English political types were exaggerated in themselves, and simply did not need a satirist to make them appear so. The form of Adams' comment here - his use of Dickens and Thackeray - is interesting in the light of his current reputation. Adams is now known primarily as a literary man and a describer of human nature, and it is clear from this chapter of the *Education* that this ability was his as a young man as it was when he was old.

Individualism Again: Under the guise of "eccentricities," Adams here investigates the situation of the individual in society, as he did in the chapter on his Harvard education. The implication is clear: in a world of conformity, anyone who insists on being an individual, who remains true to himself, runs the risk of being called an eccentric. He makes the comment that English society was generally more tolerant of eccentricity than the American, and uses his own experience as proof of this statement.

Comment: Again Adams is using his own experience as proof of a general truth, the truth that the individual occupies a precarious position in society. This, too, is an idea which Adams will take up later when he predicts that the individual will have an even harder time in the twentieth century than he had in the nineteenth. This is one of the ideas which has made the *Education* so popular for twentieth-century readers, since in so many respects this prediction of Adams' seems to have come true.

CHAPTER XIII: THE PERFECTION OF HUMAN SOCIETY

Again, the reader of Adams will recognize this title as one which will probably prove ironic, and again he will be right. Adams starts the chapter with an amusing statement on his father's now-secure position in London society. After having won "the Battle of the Rams" (described in Chapter XI), Minister Adams was firmly lodged as a force to be recognized in England. This took some of the burden off "the private secretary," and young Adams now had considerably more free time at his disposal than he had had before. In this chapter Adams considers his experiences with London social life. As usual, he evaluates himself as a failure in this field, but his accounts are predictably interesting. In his words, "his own want of experience prevented his asking introductions to the ladies who ruled society; his want of friends prevented his knowing who these ladies were; and he had every reason to expect snubbing if he put himself in evidence." Although making fun of himself specifically, Adams is here considering the predicament of the gauche American exposed to the sophisticated rigmarole of European society; Adams' own social experiences had not equipped him for a London "season," but then no young American of his day would have been able to cope with such a phenomenon.

Ironies: Adams' account of London social life is one of the funnier parts of the *Education*. He is doubly ironic; he satirizes the clumsy, inept, rather naive young man that he was, but he also satirizes the too-worldly, too-weary social lions who were his adversaries. It is interesting that Adams, without any boasting, manages to contrast his own polite naivete with the snobbery of the social elite of London. The implication is strong that the "barbaric" young American was in fact considerably better-mannered than most of the members of high society.

Adams' Friendships: Aside from being a biting statement on social custom, this chapter is again interesting for its comment on Adams' friends. As usual, he minimizes these relationships, but they are interesting nevertheless; during his London years, Adams was on friendly terms with some of the most famous Englishmen of that period.

CHAPTER XIV: DILETTANTISM

This chapter begins with an account of the Adams' brief sojourn in Italy, where the older man had been sent on account of his health. The assassination of President Lincoln occurred while they were in Rome; Adams, with characteristic sensitivity, refers to this act as an "education" for all Americans. After President Andrew Johnson assumed office, the Adams' duties were considerably diminished; and so "the private secretary" had a chance to pursue his interests in the field of art. Adams was by this time rather thoroughly disillusioned with the idea of a diplomatic career; he was not qualified for law; and so he turned to the fine arts.

Adams' Artistic Career: With his customary humor, Adams discusses the state of art and art appreciation in nineteenth-century England: "Of all supposed English tastes, that of art was the most alluring and treacherous. Once drawn into it, one had small chance of escape, for it had no center or circumference, no beginning, middle, or end, no origin, no object, and no conceivable result as education." And so, as he had done with other fields of endeavor, Adams turned away from art. He made several trips to Paris at this time, and met some literary figures there. His friends tried to persuade him to unite his artistic and journalistic interests and become an art critic, but again Adams rejected the idea. And so he continued in his twenty-seventh and twenty-eighth years, a dilettante (dabbler) in many of the arts. He did do some successful writing, articles which were accepted by the *North American Review* (the magazine which he was later to edit as a Harvard professor), but as usual the chapter closes with a wry note: "This was the result of five years in London... He had wholly lost his way. If he were ever to amount to anything, he must begin a new education, in a new place, with a new purpose."

CHAPTER XV: DARWINISM

The "new education" which Adams now took up for a time was Darwinism, the sociological-biological study which was then so popular in London. Adams considered Darwin's Law of Natural Selection (popularly referred to as the idea of the "survival of the fittest") to be interesting, and to some extent he accepted the idea. As usual, he credits himself with little originality in his acceptance of this theory, saying that he was "Darwinist because it was easier than not, for his ignorance exceeded belief, and one must know something..."

The major effect that the interest in Darwinism had was to lead Adams to a study of geology. He was interested in the idea of evolution, which he wryly describes as the "very best substitute for religion, a safe, conservative, practical, thoroughly common-law deity." As usual, Adams' skepticism kept him from thoroughly embracing any of these ideas; mere facts never satisfied him, and he could always think of questions which were not to be answered by pat theories.

This chapter ends with an account of more writing on Adams' part; though he does not here acknowledge the fact, these articles were being read by many people in the United States, and were building a considerable literary reputation for Adams back in his home.

Comment: Chapter XV closes one section of the *Education*, the section dealing with his years in Europe. After discovering that education didn't come from high school, college, or a jaunt about the Continent, Adams tried for seven years to find education somewhere in hard work. As he says, however, he was still quite unsuccessful; his only "education" so far had been his distinctly disillusioning experiences with the diplomatic and social worlds. He had also tried his hand at intellectual endeavor, and decided that he could

never be either artist or critic; he was having more success, however, in his literary attempts. Adams ends Chapter XV with the characteristically ironic statement that he had become "accustomed" to England, and that was about all. It was the extent, so far, of his education.

As usual, the reader must take Adams' comments here with considerable reservation. Although Adams denies that he was successful in any of the fields he tried, the facts speak for themselves and do not quite support him. He had been quietly successful in a diplomatic post of some sensitivity and importance; he had made friends with some of the most important figures of his day; his acquaintances insisted that he had a good deal of promise as an art critic; and his historical and political magazine articles had received much attention as they appeared.

Why then does Adams keep insisting that he had no "education" as yet? This is his comment on the society he lived in, and, ultimately, on mankind in general: men really cannot learn much of value in their lives; they are, in fact, destined to spend much of their time in completely inconsequential activities. What saves Adams from pessimism here is his wry, ironic acceptance of that fact. Unlike many people, Adams at least has the sense to realize that he is an insignificant creature; he manages to enjoy life as it is, without fooling himself about his own importance or his contribution to the world. This at least is his attitude halfway through the *Education*. By the end of the book the reader will find that Adams has progressed from irony through pessimism to stoicism; he accepts what he must, without trying to change things.

CHAPTER XVI: THE PRESS

This chapter begins with an account of the Adams' return to America. The first part deals especially with the tremendous changes which had occurred in their country since they had been gone; American society, Adams notes, had always been extremely fluid because of the democratic nature of the government. With industrialization of the country, and the tremendous influx of new populations from all over the world, things were changing even more - and, as a result, there were fewer "certitudes" that an American could depend on. In this throbbing new society Adams compares himself, "a survivor from the 1850's," to an earthworm, floundering around trying to discover where he had come from, and where he was going. Adams searched around trying to find a place for himself in this new America, but he found that the "market for educated labor" was small, even in Boston. Journalism seemed his only chance, but the opportunities for a bright young journalist were not exactly endless. Either personal or political prejudices, of himself as well as others, ruled out nearly all the really significant New York papers, and in Boston journalism almost didn't exist. So Adams went to Washington, where he eventually found a job. Here he continued to enjoy meeting the most famous political figures of his day, many of whom had been friends of his father. The chapter ends with the comment that Washington society, however formidable it might appear, seemed positively relaxing after his struggles with the socialites of London. Adams had, then, found some kind of place for himself.

CHAPTER XVII: PRESIDENT GRANT

This chapter begins on a personal note, as Adams comments on his enjoyment of his first Southern autumn in many years. He was simply enjoying himself now, renewing many acquaintances and commenting ironically on the somewhat chaotic state of Washington in the mid-nineteenth century. Adams states that he didn't work much that year, but instead simply tried to enjoy himself; he did, however, write, polish and send off for possible publication many articles which were printed in significant magazines of the time. At this point, Adams was trying hard to develop for himself a purely literary career; eventually, however, this attempt, like so many others, ended in disillusionment for him.

Grand Himself: This chapter includes a rather unflattering picture of President Grant, whom Adams considered a particularly nineteenth-century man, and whom he did not at all admire. In a particularly humorous passage close to the end of this chapter, Adams considers both President Grant, and Adams' own flirtation with Darwinian biology; that America should first have produced statesmen like Washington and Jefferson, and then an unimpressive figure like Grant, made the whole idea of evolution seem ridiculous to him.

Comment: Adams is characteristically humorous in his treatment of Grant and the opportunistic political society of Washington in the 1860's, but his essential pessimism shows clearly in this chapter. Adams, the eighteenth-century man who had so much admiration for the founders of his country, including his great-grandfather, saw nothing "even sensibly American" in Grant's administration. In other words, it wasn't even efficiently practical - it

was simply corrupt. At this point Adams indicates only that the evolution of American politics was not progressing towards a better state; eventually, he indicates strongly that America, in fact, was getting worse and worse.

CHAPTER XVIII: FREE FIGHT

The beginning of this chapter is another of Adams' comments on the loveliness of nature, which often far exceeds the loveliness of man. It is a passage which is notable for its lyricism, and marks Adams as a stylist of great versatility: "No European spring had shown him the same intermixture of delicate grace and passionate depravity that marked the Maryland May. He loved it too much, as though it were Greek and half human." There is an abrupt change at this point, as Adams goes on to consider with barely concealed disgust the scandals which convulsed Washington during the Grant administration. This chapter is especially interesting for a student of American history, for Adams considers in close detail the machinations which were going on behind the scenes of events, like Jay Gould's famous attempt to corner gold - an escapade which was still somewhat vague to most people when Adams wrote his *Education*, years after it happened. Adams knew most of the people who were most intensely involved in the scandals - Fish, Cox, Hoar, Evarts, Sumner - yet they were as mystified as he about what was transpiring.

Pessimism: The chapter develops a note of quiet pessimism: "The sum of political life was, or should have been, the attainment of a working political system. Society needed to reach it. If moral standards broke down, and machinery stopped working, new morals and machinery of some sort had to be invented.

An eternity of Grants, or even of Garfields or of Conklings or of Jay Goulds, refused to be conceived as possible." Adams is pessimistic here about the government itself, and about the major political figures of the '60s. He is also critical of the American society which had, because of its total lack of interest in politics, allowed such unsavory and unscrupulous men to gain control. Adams indicates at the end of this chapter that it was American "practicality" that was at fault. Americans, he indicates, were too materialistic to care about their own welfare a few years hence. Adams indicates that he was, at this time, still unwilling to slide into the moral laziness common to his fellow Americans; he still felt compelled to speak his political views to those who would listen, in an attempt to change a bad situation.

The chapter ends, however, not on a note of pessimism but instead on a note of amusement. Adams tells of an article which he wrote on Jay Gould and the money scandal. The article was printed in England, but gained much attention in America - exactly the fate which Adams had wished for it.

CHAPTER XIX: CHAOS

This chapter sees Adams back in London, commenting on the small degree of outward change and the great degree of internal change which Europe had undergone. Europe at first seemed delightful to Adams, after the seamy scandals which he had left behind in America. Gradually, however, he realized that London was changing just as rapidly as Washington, and that here, as elsewhere, there was no niche for an eighteenth-century man to occupy safely. Adams sought only rest and relaxation in London; he found excitement instead, a kind of excitement which he was not particularly anxious to indulge in.

Adams in this chapter reveals the "chaos" of Europe as it revealed itself to him - as a series of small shocks which, innocent enough in themselves, were undermining the structure of European life as he had known it. There were monetary scandals in London just as there had been in Washington; England seemed hypocritical in its attitude towards American politics; France seemed to be constantly threatening war with Germany.

The most serious shock of this year, however, was a personal one: his sister, to whom he had been extremely close, died of lockjaw as Adams himself watched. The blow was extreme: "The last lesson - the sum and term of education - began then." Adams goes on to comment that he had never really seen nature before this time; he had only seen her superficially, only seen the "sugar-coating" that the young man sees. "Flung suddenly in his face, with the harsh brutality of chance, the terror of the blow stayed by him thenceforth for life, until repetition made it more than the will could struggle with; more than he could call on himself to bear." Adams was seriously upset by the agonizing death of his sister; he was especially struck by the ironic difference between the ugliness of the sick-room and the beauty of the surrounding scenery, the Italian countryside bursting with the life of midsummer. Adams found himself unable to reconcile this **irony**, and he, who had been a lover and appreciator of nature, says here: "For many thousands of years, on these hills and plains, Nature had gone on sabring men and women with the same air of sensual pleasure."

War In Europe: As if Adams had not been close enough to despair when his sister died, he traveled back to England through a Europe which was at war. Adams saw no patriotic surges, only the cynicism and hypocrisy which the war brought out: soldiers marching to their deaths through the streets of

Paris, singing the Marseillaise, while the crowds along the way were too uninterested even to join in the singing.

Despair: The chapter ends, appropriately enough considering its contents, on a note of darkness and near-despair. Adams considers the limitations of the American character, which seem hopeless; he describes the typical bored, dull, American tourist, dependent on and too-indulgent of his wife and daughters. However foolish this character might seem, Adams indicates, he is at heart a perfectly fine citizen; he is simply lost in the world, longing for the America which he understands better than this mystifying Europe. "The American was to be met at every railway station in Europe, carefully explaining to every listener that the happiest day of his life would be the day when he should land on the pier at New York."

Comment: This chapter is particularly significant for its note of despair. Faced with the chance death of his sister, the purposeless war in Europe and the memory of ugly financial scandal in Washington, Adams has lost his sense of humor. He cannot view "chaos," either on a personal or national level, with irony any longer. The element which most disturbed him, the element which he found in the death and the war and the scandal, was chance - if man could not predict what would happen to him in the next week, man would be hard put to make any sense out of his life.

There is another element of interest to be found in Adams' account of his despair at his sister's death. His wife, whom he loved deeply, committed suicide unexpectedly because of a severe and long-lasting mental depression. This event shook Adams so much

that he did not even include it in the Education; in fact, he could hardly mention his wife's name even to his closest friends after the event. One can see the significance, then, when he says of his sister's death that "repetition made it more than the will could struggle with; more than he could call on himself to bear." Adams could not make sense out of his sister's accidental death; still less could he force himself to accept the senseless tragedy of his wife's suicide.

CHAPTER XX: FAILURE

In the beginning of this chapter, Adams turns to reminiscence; he recalls his first visit to Harvard College, an event that took place when he was a child of nine. This introduces the reader to a new phase of Adams' life, his position as Assistant Professor of History at Harvard. Adams took rooms in the old home of an aunt who had formerly lived in Cambridge; the Adams family tradition, obviously, was still holding fast. But the bulk of this chapter deals, not with personal or family considerations, but with Adams' ideas on how history should be taught. He refused to teach history as "dogma"; to cram meaningless facts into the heads of his students, or to teach his own partially-formed theories of history as if they were gospel. Adams is severely critical in this chapter of the way history had been taught; he accuses it of losing even its "sense of shame." He adds that history had fallen a century behind the experimental sciences, and concluded with the statement that history was now less beneficial to the student than the reading of novels by people like Walter Scott or Alexandre Dumas.

Humor: As usual, Adams is droll as well as incensed in his analysis of the history teacher's job. He charges the universities with being more conscious of their own reputations than they were of the knowledge gained by their students: "The college expected him to pass...his time in teaching the boys a few elementary dates and relations," he felt, simply so that they could get their degrees and avoid disgracing the school from which they came. Adams, on the other hand, tried to stimulate rather than inundate their minds, to interest his students in the material so that they might discover the facts for themselves. He is eminently practical in his consideration of the problems of the teacher, and his observations are as valid today as they were in 1871. He felt that the students had as their chief privilege the opportunity to discuss their interests with the professor. The professor, in turn, had the responsibility of drawing them out, of discovering those interests, of, at times, "devising schemes" to determine the trend of their thinking. He also had to contend with the problem of the large class, which militated against much free discussion. Finally, Adams concludes that "no man can instruct more than half-a-dozen students at once. The whole problem of education is one of money."

The entire chapter deals with Adams' theories of education, and with his trials as a schoolmaster. It ends on a characteristically wry note; after a strenuous season with lively students and disagreeing fellow teachers, Adams took a trip to the West. The unspoiled grandeur of Utah and Arizona convinced him that his problems of educational theory were not the major crises of the world, and he went back to the "humble tasks of schoolmaster and editor, harnessed to his cart."

CHAPTER XXI: TWENTY YEARS AFTER

From chapter twenty to chapter twenty-one, Adams has summarily skipped twenty years, the period during which he taught at Harvard and edited *The North American Review*. His stated reason for this omission is that he "stopped his education" in 1871, and in the intervening years was simply applying what he knew in an attempt to educate others. As usual, Adams indicates that he was successful in educating neither himself nor others; evidence from many of his devoted and successful students, however, indicates that he was an extremely inspiring and successful professor.

Melancholy: In this chapter Adams again takes up the problem of his own "education," this time with another trip to Europe. This material is marked by an attitude of great melancholy on the part of its writer. Although Adams does not give any tangible reason for his great depression in 1891, the reader with a knowledge of his biography can supply it: Adams' wife had committed suicide in 1885, and Adams never entirely recovered from the blow. This chapter gives the picture of a man beset by tragedies: his parents were dead, his brothers and sisters settled with their own families, even Europe he found "dreary." He comments rather bitterly on the politics of both America and Europe in this chapter, and ends on a note of extreme pessimism.

CHAPTER XXII: CHICAGO

In this chapter Adams takes up the era of fin-de-siecle, a French phrase which, literally translated, simply means "end of the century," but which has come to be applied to the peculiarly weary, pessimistic, enervated tone which pervaded much of life at the end of the nineteenth century. Adams himself was much affected by this feeling of inability to cope with reality, and describes his surroundings as a world "where not a breath stirred the idle air of education or fretted the mental torpor of self-content." Adams states that he had withdrawn almost entirely into his own company by 1893, dining alone at home and never appearing at social functions. Again, Adams does not supply the reason for his peculiar depression, but the reader knows that it was his wife's suicide which precipitated it. Adams did have a few staunch friends, among them John Hay and Cabot Lodge, whom he continued to see, but they were no longer the major political and cultural figures who had been his company in years previous. He was, practically speaking, almost a recluse.

Melancholy: This chapter, like the previous one, is melancholy in tone. If Adams was solitary, it was by necessity rather than by choice: "He loved solitude as little as others did; but he was unfit for social work, and he sank under the surface."

Travel Again: The pessimism of this chapter is not as unrelieved as that of the previous one, however. Adams acknowledges his essentially social nature here, and mentions gratefully the refusal of society to accept his withdrawal as permanent. Here he considers several trips which he took with understanding friends, trips which were intended to draw him out of his depression. He traveled through the South, to Cuba, to the **Exposition** in Chicago, to Europe again, and back eventually to America. Among other issues which interested Adams on his travels was the great monetary dispute of the '90's, the question of whether America should be on the silver or gold standard in money coinage. As usual, Adams is objective and ironic in his consideration of the monetary question; and as usual, the student can gain a clear and vivid knowledge of the issue from reading Adams' comments on it.

The **Exposition**: The chapter ends with Adams' consideration of the **exposition** in Chicago, a description which looks forward to his famous comments on the Paris **Exposition** of 1900. Predictably enough, Adams was both appalled by and drawn to the industrial might which he saw at the Exposition; he was becoming intensely aware that America would be a "land of the masses," and was becoming convinced that the day of the individual was passing.

The Chicago **Exposition** also impressed on him strongly the sheer physical size of America; such gigantic phenomena as Niagara Falls, the Grand Canyon, the Yellowstone Geyser, he found almost overpowering. Again, Adams concludes that this magnitude of America would militate against the status of the individual. In a place so large, man must work in groups in order not to be completely dwarfed and overpowered. The chapter concludes by uniting its two major themes, the monetary issue and the Chicago **Exposition**. Adams concludes that he, and everyone else, must accept the unpleasant fact that America will become a capitalistic "class" society, in which the law of the masses and the law of the bankers would struggle for domination. Adams is not pleased by this mass society which he visualizes, but he sees it as an inescapable fact which must be realized.

Comment: In this chapter Adams makes one of his most forceful statements on the government which he saw, and one of his most accurate predictions for the future. He sees himself as antiquated, a throwback to the eighteenth century. Rather than the government of statesmen, of individuals, which his father and grandfather represented, he predicts a government of "machinery." The acceptance of the new monetary standard was to him a symbol of the coming capitalism in America; it represented "the whole mechanical consolidation of force." If the gold standard was to him the symbol of capitalism, then

the Chicago Exposition was the symbol of the new energies of America, the great forces of machinery and industrialization which were shaping the country. This chapter ends on a pessimistic note, but it is much more controlled than the pessimism of the previous chapter; Adams stoically accepts what he sees as inevitable, even if it means the end of himself and of what he represents.

THE EDUCATION OF HENRY ADAMS

TEXTUAL ANALYSIS

CHAPTERS 23-35

....

CHAPTER XXIII: SILENCE

Here Adams ruefully takes up the problem which he had mentioned in Chapter Twenty - money. It is particularly ironic that Adams should be beset by financial problems, since he came from such a wealthy and prominent family; but again, the late nineteenth century no longer allowed for mere inherited wealth. His financial holdings had been jeopardized by bank troubles, and it was simple chance that saved him; the experience, however, made him intensely aware of what wealth was, and of how many kinds of influence money could wield. Again, Adams is eminently practical; he examines the connection between money and respect in American society, and comes to the conclusion that respect and success can be achieved only if the individual also has wealth. Adams' objectivity is particularly evident here, since he himself had both money and social position; he considers himself only little, however, and concentrates instead on some of the other, newly significant families that had gained wealth in the '90s.

In this chapter Adams also tells of travels, this time another trip to Cuba. Adams was fascinated with the semi-civilized lands that he visited; he describes Cuba as a land "which had never been fairly involved in the general motion, and was the more amusing for its torpor." Here again one can see Adams' concern with the mechanization which the nineteenth century represents; he calls civilization "motion," and is intrigued by the very laziness or "torpor" which had so far kept Cuba and other similar places out of the maelstrom of capitalism and mass society.

Europe Again: The last part of the chapter deals with another trip to Europe, this time with the Cabot Lodge family. The Lodges were great friends of Adams, and he enjoyed their visit to Europe; their point of view was congenial to his, and he felt less depressed than he had when he saw Europe alone. This chapter closes on a more optimistic note than the previous one had, though this emotion is controlled; Adams' acceptance of the world in which he lived is more nearly complete. "For the old world of public men and measures since 1870, Adams wept no tears. Within or without, during or after it, as partisan or historian, he never saw anything to admire in it, or anything he wanted to save..." Adams is no longer lamenting the world which came to an end in the '70s; he accepts, if ruefully, the fact that the world of twenty years ago was a mediocre and lackluster place, even as the world of the '90s is. He is not particularly fond of the turn-of-the-century world of Europe and America, but he accepts it.

Serenity: The chapter ends on a quieter, more placid note than Adams' writing in this section of the *Education* has given evidence of. He discusses his trip to Egypt to see his friend John Hay; together, they drift down the Nile, viewing the Egyptian ruins and archeological discoveries, they go to Constantinople to see the ruins there. The reader senses here that Adams' mind is as relaxed as his trip was; he is drifting through the great scenes of antiquity, and this puts the present in a more tolerable perspective.

CHAPTER XXIV: INDIAN SUMMER

In this chapter Adams considers the "Indian summer" of his life, his sixtieth year. Again he seems serene and ready to accept life on its own terms, asking for no more than time and quiet to reflect on the past events of his life. There is a sharp contrast between Adams' serenity and the state of the world in 1898, for this was the beginning of the Spanish-American War. Adams seems resigned and somewhat distant in his consideration of this war; he is no longer appalled, as he was at times during the Civil War, but rather seems to think that battles are a quite predictable activity of mankind. He looks back over the two-hundred year history of America, and concludes that the Spanish-American War was simply another "stage" in history, and not something which one could become excited about. Part of the "removal" which ones senses here comes from Adams' consideration of himself, not as Henry Adams, but as the late-nineteenth century representative of his family; they had long predicted the kind of struggle in which America found itself in 1898, and Adams considers this fact a rather bitter vindication of one hundred and fifty years of Adams political opinion. Another reason for his "removal" is that Adams was an American who was acquainted with the Philippines and Puerto Rico, two of the objects of the Spanish-American War. He understood thoroughly, then, the causes of the war, the war itself, and many possible outcomes which could be predicted to come of it.

Two American Types: As usual, Adams considers both national and personal activities in this chapter; he ends it with a description of his friends John LaFarge and John Hay. He considers these two men as representative types: LaFarge, the artist, who insists on individuality and who removes himself from the turmoil of current events, and Hay, the political man to whom current affairs are life's blood. Hay also represents something else to Adams in this chapter; he was responsible for bringing about a new mathematical interest in Adams. Adams compares Kepler and Newton, and the "liberties" they took with astronomical laws - in order to prove new laws - to nineteenth-century politicians, who took "liberties" with civic laws and with people, in order to achieve political successes. Adams grants the mathematicians and the politicians the right to do as they wish, but it is evident that his sympathies are not with these experimenters. The chapter ends with another of Adams' comparisons of progress in civilization with progress in mathematics. Adams implies that politicians should see the difference between people and mathematical laws: "History had no use for multiplicity; it needed unity... Everything must be made to move together."

> **Comment: This chapter is significant for what it indicates about Adams' attitude toward the world. The deep pessimism, almost despair, which began in chapter XXI has been tempered gradually; by Chapter XXIV what was despair, then stoical acceptance, has become resignation. Adams has withstood personal tragedy; he has looked at the national tragedies of war and political double-dealing; he has observed the growth of capitalism and mass society, forms of life which are antithetical to all that he represents. He does not pretend that these phenomena appeal to him, but he accepts what he considers inevitable. Chapter XXIV ends with something very much like a plea for change: don't pretend to be mathematicians,**

he tells the politicians, but realize that you are dealing with people. There is little indication that Adams thinks his plea will be heard. The fact that he can still express it, however, indicates that he is no longer plunged into despair.

CHAPTER XXV: THE DYNAMO AND THE VIRGIN

In this chapter Adams takes up his visit to another **Exposition**, the famous Paris **Exposition** of 1900, in which the great dynamos were unveiled before the eyes of the masses. Adams begins the chapter with a brief account of the scientific advancement since the seventeenth century; he indicates that anyone who knew about Francis Bacon should have been prepared for the dynamos of 1900. Adams himself was not, however; he understood neither the principle behind the dynamos nor the uses to which they would be put. At this point Adams is again highly ironic about his education: that he, a man as well educated as anyone of his age, should be in total darkness as to the dynamo, the most important fact of the twentieth century, struck him as bitterly funny. Neither his school nor his life had prepared him for the dynamo. He was struck dumb, and paralyzed by this new and overwhelming force.

Force: The entire Paris **Exposition** was devoted to a study of force: the motors which would eventually drive the automobiles and airplanes, and the dynamo, which represented a force which could rival the sun. Adams' own words are the best description of what the dynamo represented to him: "To Adams the dynamo had become a symbol of infinity." After frequent visits to the great gallery of machines, Adams eventually began to consider the forty-foot dynamos as a moral force, "much as the early Christians felt the Cross." This new force was almost beyond measurement: "The planet itself seemed less impressive, in its old-fashioned, deliberate, annual or daily revolution, than this huge wheel, revolving...at some vertiginous speed, and barely murmuring...while it would not wake the baby lying close to its frame." Adams mockingly compares himself with the men who made and understood the dynamos, and who saw them simply as a very practical means of power, of driving machines or carrying people from one place to another. These scientists, Adams ruefully predicts, will eventually be the elite; in the twentieth century they will, like the ancient shaman or witch doctor, be the only ones to understand the forces which rule the life of their time.

The Terrifying Mystery: It is exactly the mystery of the dynamos which most impressed - and most terrified - Adams. He could understand the simple little engine whose working parts were visible, and whose energy was limited. It was the secrecy of the dynamos, their "occult mechanisms," the incomprehensible magnitude of their power, which made him see them as the new religious force. The ordinary man could never understand the new source of power; he could never conceive what supplied him with the things he lived by; and so he was in the same position as the earliest Christian, who had to live by faith in what his priest told him. Adams also considered the dynamo a symbol to the twentieth-century man, just as the Cross and the cathedral had been symbols to the medieval Christian. Mere arithmetic, and the older sciences, had been replaced; the twentieth-century man must simply accept "an absolute fiat in electricity as in faith." He must, then, accept the world of the modern scientist and the value of the symbolic machines which they perfected; he would no longer understand the primary forces of his life.

The Position Of The Historian: As usual, Adams interprets this new knowledge as it will affect himself as historian. The dynamos would destroy the historian, he predicted, since historians are constantly involved in figuring out cause-and-effect relationships. The dynamo, because it is incomprehensible, is unpredictable; the force which it produces seems to be totally unrelated to its source. Neither force nor source is measurable; and so cause and effect will be meaningless in the twentieth-century world. With characteristic **irony** Adams describes himself after his confrontation with the greatest machines: "...thus it happened that, after ten years' pursuit, he found himself lying in the Gallery of Machines at the Great **Exposition** of 1900, his historical neck broken by the sudden irruption of forces totally new."

The New Religion: In the last half of this chapter Adams develops his idea of the dynamo as the new religion. He compares the sterile, mechanistic power produced by the dynamo to the fertile, productive power represented by the old Christian symbol, the Virgin who had inspired the builders of such magnificent cathedrals as that at Chartres. As an antidote to the hall of dynamos, Adams haunted the Paris art galleries, looking at the famous and beautiful paintings, of Madonnas and Virgins which hung there. The Virgin, he saw, represented productivity and intuition and humanity. She had been a humanizing force, a symbol of life and creation; in Adams' opinion, the Virgin, both in pagan and Christian religions, had been the symbol which kept mankind whole and civilized. He concludes the chapter by indicating that the new symbolic force, the dynamo, would render man's imagination sterile and make his life meaningless; he predicts, in effect, the era of mechanized man.

Comment: This chapter is perhaps the most famous and most-quoted section of the entire *Education*. It, along with the previous chapter, explains why Adams described the book as "a study in twentieth-century

multiplicity." Adams sees mechanistic force as overwhelming the twentieth century. He also predicts that this force will divide men from men, will make the studies of such fields as history meaningless, will replace art with science. Against the symbol of the dynamo he puts the symbol of the Virgin, both the Christian Virgin Mary and the many virgin-fertility symbols which can be found in almost all pagan religions. The Virgin held men together, Adams indicates; and he points to such massive constructions as the French cathedrals as evidence of this fact. The implication of this chapter is that men, who had been held together by their acceptance of symbols of unity, love, and new life, would be divided by their new and necessary allegiance to the mysterious, sterile force of the dynamo. The picture for the twentieth-century man, then, is not an especially happy one. Adams does not sound despairing, however; he simply presents facts and his own conclusions, and leaves the reader to draw the significance for himself.

CHAPTER XXVI: TWILIGHT

In this chapter Adams leaves the world of machinery for another world, more familiar to him: he writes of the political machinations then going on in Asia. Again, Adams' ability to predict the future seems almost uncanny to the modern reader; he considers the goings-on in Peking, the struggle in 1901 for the control of China, to be the most significant event of the decade. He calls the politicians obtuse because of their failure to realize the significance of China to the world as a whole: "The value of a Ming vase was more serious than universal war." The modern reader can appreciate the wisdom of Adams' judgments; the fate of China now seems to all to be a deciding force in the fate of the world.

Unlike the chapter on the Virgin and the Dynamo, this one deals primarily with purely political situations. Again Adams views the world of current affairs through his friends and acquaintances; he traces China's history at this time through the activities of John Hay, who was much responsible for the outcome of the negotiations. Again, this chapter gives an interesting account of nineteenth-century history; Adams' approach to this political situation, like others, is fresh and objective.

The Death Of A Friend: The chapter ends, however, on another note of personal sadness. Adams' good friend King, who had also been involved in the China negotiations, died suddenly, partly as a result of his exhausting work. Adams comments on his and Hay's reactions to the tragedy, and again the reader is aware of what Adams does not mention specifically: Adams was even more struck by the death than Hay, also a good friend of King's, because Adams was so alone, so deprived of immediate family since the death of his wife.

CHAPTER XXVII: TEUFELSDROCKH

Adams is in Paris again at the beginning of this chapter, touring the art galleries; theatres and cathedrals. The reader senses Adams' feeling of relief; Paris is "still Paris," despite the upheavals taking place in China. The world of art was flourishing in Paris, and Adams was able to lose himself, at least for a time, in a world other than the unfriendly and frightening one of power politics. While in Paris he met his friends the Cabot Lodges, who took him off to Germany, where he visited many of the towns he had seen as a much younger man, on his first tour of Europe. Among other things, he took in the Wagner festival at Bayreuth, but the magnificence of the German's operas was lost on Adams. He was aware only of the insignificance of the music, in comparison with what was going on in the world.

Order And Disorder: The experience in Bayreuth leads Adams back to one of his favorite theories, the differences between order and unity, and disorder and disunity. He compares the orderly world of music, even the sometimes-emotional notes of Wagner, with the seeming chaos of the contemporary world. He goes on to draw parallels between music and philosophy, and the arts.

Russia: Adams' pessimism asserts itself again in this chapter. The idea that synthesis, or unity, is the end of philosophy, is an optimistic one, since it implies that this order is attainable. Adams goes on to say, however, that the whole question of synthesis is purely an academic one; that finally, synthesis and anarchy are one, since there is no such thing as true order. He sees this theory as being in part the product of Hegel, the German nineteenth-century philosopher whose influence was beginning to be strongly felt in Europe. Adams was studying Hegel in preparation for his trip to Russia, where he went after his stay in Germany. Adams realized that Hegel and Russia were closely connected. Adams was especially struck by Russia, which he had never seen before. The country and its people seemed primeval to him, and unchangeable. Russia was totally foreign to him, who was so much a child of the West. He ends the chapter with another look at Germany, in comparison with Russia. He comments that Germany seemed then very much like America, in its industrialization and sophistication; Russia appears like an unknown quantity still, waiting in mystery at the other end of Europe.

CHAPTER XXVIII: THE HEIGHT OF KNOWLEDGE

Adams discusses 1901 as a "year of tragedy" because of political misfortunes, and because of the death of friends which took place in that year. His friend John Hay lost both his son and his father that year; Adams, ever sensitive to such personal tragedy, took his friend's losses hard, and the deaths cast a gloom over the beginning of 1902. The mood of pessimism is again reflected in this chapter; Adams discusses the political career of Theodore Roosevelt as a study in opportunism, a quality which he abhorred in public figures. He is particularly interested here in the effects of power on the individual personality, and is blunt in his conclusion: "Power is poison." It is this power, he implies, which turns Roosevelt, basically an honest and direct man, into a conniver. As Adams says, "The effect of unlimited power on limited minds is worth noting in Presidents because it must represent the same process in society, and the power of self-control must have a limit somewhere in face of control of the infinite."

Roosevelt And Cabot Lodge: In this chapter Adams also discusses the difference between the natural man-Roosevelt-and the educated man-Cabot Lodge. Roosevelt, he asserts, was what he was simply because of his temperament and nature; Lodge, on the other hand, represented the same laborious "educational" process which Adams himself had undergone. Adams is particularly interested in Lodge's awareness of his past and the past of his country, in contrast to Roosevelt's interest in the moment, as if there were no such thing as tradition.

The chapter concludes with another of Adams' statements on forces in political life: "Modern politics is, at bottom, a struggle not of men but of forces. The men become every year more and more creatures of force, massed about central powerhouses. The conflict is no longer between men, but between the motors that drive the men, and the men tend to succumb to their own motive forces."

> **Comment: The parallel between Adams' ideas of political force and the force of the dynamos here is obvious. He is saying again that the individual is lost, that society, like industry, will in the modern world be driven by mysterious and uncontrollable forces which man can neither understand nor cope with.**

CHAPTER XXIX: THE ABYSS OF IGNORANCE

The beginning of this chapter again sees Adams traveling about Europe, visiting friends in Scotland, Paris, Switzerland and Germany. The tone here is again serene, as if Adams has digested and accepted the conclusions which he presented. Adams tells us that "Life at last managed of its own accord to settle itself into a working arrangement. After so many years of effort to find one's drift, the drift found the seeker, and slowly swept him forward and back, with a steady progress oceanwards." Adams is drifting about Europe, then, much as he had drifted about Egypt in Chapter Twenty-three; again he views society with a calm, if not a particularly happy, eye. He is still interested in the mystery of force, however, and discusses what the nineteenth-century French philosopher Pascal called "the inability to sit still." Adams considers here Pascal's statement that half the world's problems stem simply from man's restlessness, a nervous energy which forces action whether or not it is constructive. Adams considers this theory; he also visits more of his beloved cathedrals, and considers again the force represented by the Virgin and by the Christian church itself. He briefly considers medieval philosophy here, since that philosophy, like Adams, was much concerned with the necessity of unity and order in man's life; he finds, however, none of the answers which the thirteenth-century philosophers had considered acceptable. Adams is like the modern man of literature in this chapter; he is beset by doubts even when he would like to believe; the power of faith is denied him wherever he seeks it, in art, or religion, or science itself.

A Possible Answer: In this chapter, however, Adams suggests for himself at least a limited answer to his questions. It is at the end of this chapter that he begins to develop his cyclical notion of history: that there are high points in man's history, points at which, for a variety of reasons, man can have a high opinion of himself and his orderly universe; there are also corresponding low points, when man can only despair. Adams fixes the dates 1150--1250 as the highest point, represented by "Amiens Cathedral and the works of Thomas Aquinas"; and he indicates that the motion has been downward since that time. It was in Paris in this year of 1902, he tells the reader, that he conceived the idea of writing one book, *Mont-Saint-Michel and Chartres: a Study in Thirteenth-Century Unity*, and another, *The Education of Henry Adams: a Study of Twentieth-Century Multiplicity*. This chapter ends thus, on a somewhat positive note: after having worked out this historical concept for himself, and after resolving to write the two books, he set home in a more optimistic frame of mind than he had been in for some time.

CHAPTER XXX: VIS INERTIAE

The beginning of this chapter continues Adams' evaluation of Roosevelt. He is interested in Roosevelt's achievements in foreign affairs, though he does not exaggerate their effectiveness. He does, however, say that Roosevelt at least saw something to be gained from skillful handling of foreign affairs, where many of his contemporaries did not. China, and its openness to the West, was still the major issue in 1903, and many political careers-John Hay's included-hung on the decision which China would make.

Richness Of Detail: This is another of the numerous chapters which are interesting for their richness of small, intimate, political detail. Adams pictures the entire list of forces aligned on the Chinese question: America, France, Germany, England, Russia. In Adams' own words, "whole continents of study" were opened by the political in-fighting on the Chinese question. The problem of Russia was especially interesting to the historian or political observer in 1903, since Russia had only fairly recently been considered a European power; few of the observers in the West knew whether Russia considered herself of the East or West. Again, Adams is fascinated by "the enigma of Russia"; the kind of power which Russia exerted was of particular interest to him, with his view of history as forces and counterforces interacting. He contrasts the "inertia" of Russia to the nervous activity of the United States: "When Russia rolled over a neighboring people, she absorbed their energies in her own movement of custom and race which neither Czar nor peasant could convert...into any western equivalent." Again Adams seems prophetic in his statements about Russia and China: "The vast force of inertia known as China was to be united with the huge bulk of Russia in a single mass which no amount of new force could henceforward deflect." This union of Russia and China did not happen precisely as Adams saw it in 1903; the student of the 1960's, however, knows that something rather similar has happened since then.

These reflections on the nature of countries and races lead Adams to a consideration of the American temperament, particularly the nature of American women. Adams had always enjoyed the company of women in society, and he considered their intuitive, unreflective opinions often more accurate than the cautioned, reasoned opinions of men. At the end of the chapter he considers Woman as a symbol rather similar to the Virgin; the Church, which Adams considered feminine, had been replaced by science, and Adams saw the possibility of woman's instinctive wisdom being replaced by the more sterile, rational knowledge of men.

CHAPTER XXXI: THE GRAMMAR OF SCIENCE

The title of this chapter is the title of a book which Adams read in pursuing his study of the differences between the sexes and the races, and of the different types of energy and inertia of which each sex or race could give evidence. "The Grammar of Science," by Karl Pearson, was a treatise which interpreted history in scientific and mathematical terms; Adams confesses to ignorance of many of Pearson's mathematical principles, but he was fascinated by the conclusions which Pearson drew. Among other things, Pearson indicated that Chaos, not Order, was the natural end of science and of man: "In plain words, Chaos was the law of nature; Order was the dream of man." Pearson drew his conclusions from study of the actions of the gases in the universe; Adams had come to a very similar conclusion (which he evidenced in the preceding chapters) from his observations of the actions of man.

Satire: Adams is rather satirical in his discussion of the sciences in this chapter-he trusted the words of scientists as little as he trusted anything else-but he considered Pearson's statements about Chaos as aptly descriptive of the world in 1900. The forces of Chaos had been in motion for years, he states, but things came to a **climax** "when, in 1898, Mme. Curie threw...the **metaphysical** bomb called radium. There remained no hole to hide in." It was with the discovery of radium, Adams indicates, and with other scientific discoveries resulting from the Curies' experiments, that the age of Chaos was formally ushered in.

> **Comment: Again, the student in the '60s cannot help feeling that Adams was prophetic in his ideas of disorder, and in his calling the discovery of radium a "metaphysical bomb." The twentieth century has been the age of science, the age in which incredible discoveries were made and in which unbelievable scientific advancements took place. It has also been, however, an age in which faith has had a hard time of it. This seems to be one of the major reasons Adams has been such a popular writer during the middle years of this century; it has become commonplace for modern writers to call this an age of science or an age of sterility or an age of disorder, but Adams' insights, in the early 1900's, are amazing. It is also interesting to note that he does not despair when he reaches unpleasant conclusions; he always accepts the reality which he sees.**

CHAPTER XXXII: VIS NOVA

This chapter begins on a note of serenity and acceptance. Adams is in Paris in midsummer, when many of the city's inhabitants have retreated to the country to escape the heat. However, Adams knew no place where history might be better pursued than in the quiet of Paris; he steeped himself in the tradition-laden atmosphere of such places as the Champs Elysees, where he could meditate calmly on the political convulsions seizing the world. Again the lands of the East were of primary interest to the statesmen of the West; Japan and Manchuria and Russia were threatening war daily, and no one knew which way events would go. Adams is understandably cynical in his treatment of the deluge of rumors which overwhelmed Europe; from day to day, supposedly informed men would tell the world that there would be war, there would be no war, again that there would be war. Eventually Adams returned to Washington, where rumors were also rampant; among other things, Adams was amused at the Americans' new interest in Russia, since he had been aware of that country's significance several years before.

The St. Louis **Exposition**: Still another exposition is accounted for in this chapter. Adams visited the St. Louis **Exposition** in 1903, and is cynical in the extreme in his view of its accomplishments. "One saw here a third-rate town of half-a-million people without history, education, unity, or art, and with little capital...but doing what London, Paris or New York would have shrunk from attempting. This new social conglomeration with no tie but its steam-power and not much of that, threw away thirty or forty million dollars on a pageant as ephemeral as a stage flat." Adams gives a stinging indictment of the tasteless, garish display he saw at St. Louis; one senses his longing for tradition, for history, for some kind of artistic sense. What he found instead was wasted talent and wasted money, and an extremely discouraging idea of the future of America.

A Contrast: Adams contrasts the tasteless mediocrity of St. Louis with a somewhat older **exposition** - the festival which was put on in the year 1250 in the town of Coutances in Normandy. This "**Exposition**" was a religious gathering in honor of the Virgin, and Adams' point of contrast is plain.

A religious festival in the thirteenth century was an honest expression of deep emotion on the part of the people, whereas the **expositions** in twentieth-century America were simply expensive tourist-traps.

CHAPTER XXXIII: A DYNAMIC THEORY OF HISTORY

In this chapter, Adams develops at some length his view of history as the result of different forces which act and react on one another. Adams states that he sees the forces of nature capturing man; man, a feeble individual, cannot resist the massed natural forces which attack and eventually overpower him. Adams develops an image to explain his position: he likens man to a spider in its web, waiting for some kind of prey. The forces of nature are like the flies before the spider's net; the spider leaps at them when possible, but it can make mistakes even when it seems to be operating on sound principles. He likens man's mind to the mind of the spider; the insect, like man, has learned a certain routine knowledge which enables him to build skillful webs and trap his prey; but he has learned nothing else. Man, too, in Adams' view, has learned things from nature; he has learned about fire, water, motion, and how to put animals to his own use. Adams then says that man's real education was complete long before the dawn of history, since all that man can really learn is this kind of natural lore. He gained his knowledge from natural phenomena, but they in turn are constantly shaping him, without his awareness. For a time, Adams goes on, man used the symbol of God to represent those natural forces which he controlled and in turn was controlled by; scientific discoveries, however, reduced the powers of what man had called God, and so man put science into the place of God. Adams defines religion as "cultivation of occult force"; he defines science in the same way.

The Cross And Science: Adams explains his theory at some length, and gives different examples of man's behavior in varying stages of his development. The central and most significant fact of his theory, however, is this: "A dynamic law requires that two masses - nature and man - must go on, reacting upon each other, without any stop, as the sun and a comet react on each other, and that any appearance of stoppage is illusive." During all the years of Christianity, Adams continues, the Cross represented one force around which man could rally; and to an extent, he had some defense against the forces of nature. He uses the Roman Empire as an example of a powerful organization which used the force of the Cross in a physical and spiritual sense, and contrasts it to the powers of Eastern Christendom, represented by Constantinople. These powers, Adams asserts, were a more complicated phenomenon; they were less dependent on religion and more dependent on science. Adams continues tracing the religious history of Europe, until "new forces, chemical and mechanical, grew in volume until they acquired sufficient mass to take the place of the old religious science." Now in the twentieth century, he concludes, man follows science as he once followed the Cross; the symbolic value is different, however, since science is the god of reason, analysis and disunity, while the Cross represented the Virgin, intuition, life and unity.

Comment: This idea of history is a highly complex one, a theory which has been accepted by many but which has drawn argument from many others. Adams does not preach his theory, however; he does not insist that everyone else accept what he believes. He simply has worked out an idea that is meaningful to him, one which explains successfully, to him at least, the phenomena of history. Presented by Adams, the "dynamic theory of history" as a

series of reacting forces seems reasonable; it was not put forth, however, as an argument to convince others, but simply as a working-out of the historical events as they appeared to Adams. The student would be wise, in an evaluation of Adams' theory, to consult other conflicting views and see how they are presented.

CHAPTER XXXIV: A LAW OF ACCELERATION

In this chapter Adams continues the theory presented in the previous one, giving examples from the natural world to illuminate his idea of the workings of man's world. He views man's activities in terms of the use of energy, and indicates that great quantities of energy had been consumed, and great forces were set in motion, with the scientific advances of the nineteenth and early twentieth centuries. He views history as a process of gradual acceleration, then; man progressed slowly during the first centuries of his life on earth, but has been proceeding ever more rapidly as time goes on. One of the major problems for the twentieth century, Adams predicts, will be this very speed of progress. Man will continue to grow scientifically much faster than his "spider-mind" can assimilate his own advances; eventually, then, man's technological knowledge may outstrip his understanding of himself and his activities. "Eventually the new American would need to think in contradictions, and...the new universe would know no law that could not be proved by its anti-law." Adams concludes this chapter with a note of very controlled optimism: "thought...must enter a new phase subject to new laws. Thus far, since five or ten thousand years, the mind had successfully reacted, and nothing yet proved that it would fail to react-but it would need to jump."

CHAPTER XXXV: NUNC AGE

This final chapter of the *Education* begins on a note of reminiscence; it is now forty years, Adams says, since he returned to New York after beginning his "education" as his father's private secretary in England. He comments on the drastic changes New York has seen since he entered it in the mid-nineteenth century; what was then just a fairly large city has become a metropolis exploding in all directions. He briefly compares the new New York to Rome under the emperor Diocletian, "witnessing the anarchy, conscious of compulsion, eager for the solution, but unable to conceive whence the next impulse was to come or how it was to act." The old world that Adams knew is dying, then, just as the old Roman Empire died; Adams sees himself in this chapter as a citizen of that old world, out of place in the new and probably not understood by the new men. The chapter concludes with references to *Hamlet*; Adams, like Hamlet, considers himself to be living in a time that is "out of joint," a time that he understands little. He concludes with a mention of the death of John Hay, one of his best friends. Adams too is ill, and he senses that his own death is imminent, as well as the death of the world he knew.

THE EDUCATION OF HENRY ADAMS

ESSAY QUESTIONS AND ANSWERS

Question: In what sense could Henry Adams be considered a Hamlet figure?

Answer: Most significantly, Adams himself chooses to end his *Education* with a mention of Hamlet's silence in the midst of noise and gaiety; therefore; Adams himself makes the comparison. But there are many points of similarity which the reader can deduce for himself. Adams, like Hamlet, was a highly introspective individual, much given to long meditations on the problems which confronted him. Although the man Adams was known to be fond of society, the speaker that one finds in the *Education* is quiet, withdrawn, and meditative, much like *Hamlet*. Adams is also given to soliloquies, or long periods of vocal soul-searching-in a very real sense, the entire *Education* can be considered an extended soliloquy on Adams' view of society. Most importantly, perhaps, both Adams and Hamlet were extremely dissatisfied with the times in which they lived; Hamlet declared "the time is out of joint," and Adams wrote the whole *Education* to make the point that the nineteenth century was out of joint, and that the twentieth century would probably be worse.

There is one major difference between Adams and Hamlet, a difference which should be noted. By the end of his play, Hamlet finds courage and initiative enough to act, and act violently. Adams never does; he remains meditative and philosophical about what he saw. But on the whole, the speaker whom one finds in the *Education* can quite justifiably be compared to *Hamlet*.

Question: Can one trust the speaker of *The Education of Henry Adams* completely? That is, does Adams reveal his entire personality in the work?

Answer: No, Adams makes no pretense of revealing his whole personality, of stripping himself naked before the world. In fact, he attached a "Preface" to the *Education* in which he states that he is revealing a "manikin," the public person rather than the interior one. *The Education* in one sense is quite impersonal; Adams obviously intends it to be a reflection of the age at least as much as it is a reflection of any person. Then, too, the individual who knows Adams' biography realizes that there were many details of his private life which he simply chose to omit - most significantly, the suicide of his wife in 1885. This is quite justifiable, of course, considering the purpose for which Adams wrote the book. He did not intend to write a "confession," but simply to reveal his times through the eyes of an objective but interested observer.

Question: How does Adams achieve the great objectivity which is one of the characteristics of the *Education*?

Answer: The most obvious source of this objectivity and apparent lack of interest is Adams' choice of third person rather than first person to write in. Because of this interesting technique, the reader is aware of Adams as a character, not as the man to whom all the events happened. Adams' **irony** also puts him at a distance from his material; he is able to view even things which affected him personally through the lens of humor, almost as if they had happened to someone else.

Question: In what sense can Adams, who lived in the nineteenth century, be considered a modern man?

Answer: Adams is in many ways a familiar figure in the mid-twentieth century. For one thing, one sees in Adams the sense of isolation which one has learned to expect in modern times. He states often and at length that he was a man out of his time, a man intended for the eighteenth century but living in the nineteenth. He is also somewhat isolated psychologically, even though he had many friends; his wife died more than thirty years before he did, and he had no children or close family after her death.

Adams also predicted the kind of emotional weariness and sterility which one finds in the twentieth century, especially in its literature. With his choice of the dynamo as the symbol of the modern age, Adams put his finger on one of the things which has most plagued his followers, the mechanization of living and the resultant impersonality of man's relationship to his fellow man. Adams also predicted a phenomenon which we have come to live with, however little we like it: the age of science, the age in which man is able to produce tremendous force, but is seemingly not able to control it. If Adams seems very much the modern man, then, it is because he predicted, in many cases, the kind of world and society in which modern man lives.

Question: Should one accept at face value Adams' estimation of himself as a man who never received an education, a man who was in many cases a failure?

Answer: Definitely not. Adams' ironic and self-effacing view of himself is one of the most interesting characteristics of the *Education*, but the reader must weigh Adams' own comments against the facts, and against the comments of his contemporaries. Adams was for twenty years a teacher of history at Harvard University; he was on friendly terms with some of the most significant figures of his age, both in America and Europe; he was a writer of importance, and his History is unrivaled in America. Many of his students credit him with being an inspiring and influential teacher, a man who changed pedagogical method in one of the most influential universities in the country. He is still read today, and his theory of history still occasions discussion. By any standards, Adams is not a failure. What is interesting about his self-evaluation is what it reveals about man - Adams is simply saying, as many men have said before, that earthly goals are necessarily limited, and that even a famous man can be beset by melancholy and self-doubt. This is, in fact, one of the great humanizing influences in the book. It puts Adams, a "Boston Brahmin" and a member of the social elite, on the level of the common man. The self-effacement of the *Education* is one of the reasons it is such a significant work.

Question: Is Adams a pessimist?

Answer: Adams is a pessimist, but only in a limited sense. He saw history as a series of endless crises, of forces pitting themselves against forces, with no relief - but he does not present this as cause for despair. Instead, Adams himself remained interested in the phenomenon called man, and his attitude appears to be more one of reserved skepticism and stoicism, rather than a despairing pessimism.

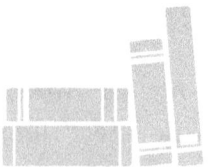

BIBLIOGRAPHY

Adams, Henry. *A Cycle of Adams Letters*. Ed. Worthington C. Ford. Boston, 1920. Family letters exchanged during the Civil War, showing young Adams' aptitude for diplomacy.

_____. *Democracy*. New York, 1961. Popular political novel published anonymously in 1880.

_____. *Esther - A Novel*. New York, 1884. Published under pseudonym, Frances Snow Compton; concerns woman's search for spiritual truth.

_____. *Henry Adams and His Friends*. ed. Harold Dean Cater. Boston, 1907. 600 letters to close friends; helps balance the picture presented by *the Education*.

_____. *Letters of Henry Adams*. ed. Worthington C. Ford. Boston, 1930. Limited in scope, but indispensable for serious knowledge of Adams' life and attitudes.

_____. *Mont-Saint-Michel and Chartres*. New York, 1959. Important for full understanding of Adams' philosophy.

_____. *The Selected Letters of Henry Adams*. New York, 1951. Convenient and most rewarding selection of letters.

Amory, Cleveland. *The Proper Bostonians*. New York, 1947. Readable, if somewhat popularized, account of the society Adams knew.

Baym, Max I. *The French Education of Henry Adams*. New York, 1951. Interesting study of Adams' investigation of French historians and philosophers.

Beringause, Arthur R. *Brooks Adams*. New York, 1955. Well-documented study dealing with the intellectual interplay between Henry Adams and his brother.

Blackmur, R. P. *The Lion and the Honeycomb*. New York, 1955. Contains provocative article on *the Education*.

_____. "The Harmony of True Liberalism," *Sewanee Review* (Winter, 1952). Penetrating analysis of the philosophy revealed in *Chartres*.

_____. "The Novels of Henry Adams," *Sewanee Review* (Spring 1943). Appraisal of Adams' artistry and politics.

Blanck, Jacob, *Bibliography of American Literature*. New Haven, 1955. Most descriptive bibliography of Adams' writings.

Commager, Henry Steele. "Henry Adams," in Marcus W. Jenegan *Essays in American* Historiography, ed. William T. Hutchinson. New York, 1948. Illuminating study of Adams as historian.

Hochfield, George. *Henry Adams: An Introduction and Interpretation*. New York, 1962. Informative introduction to Adams' thought.

Hume, Robert. *Runaway Star: An Appreciation of Henry Adams*. Ithaca, New York, 1951. Study of Adams' qualities as an individual.

Jones, Howard Mumford. *The Theory of American Literature.* Ithaca, New York, 1948. Relates Adams' writings to American literature in a general way.

Jordy, William H. *Henry Adams: Scientific Historian.* New Haven, 1952. Penetrating analysis of Adams' use of contemporary science in his theory of history.

Levenson, J. C. *The Mind and Art of Henry Adams.* Boston, 1957. Full and perceptive study of Adams as artist and thinker; particularly good on *the Education* and *Chartres.*

Lovett, Robert N. "The Betrayal of Henry Adams," Dial, LXV (1918), 468–72. *Review of Education* at time of publication; useful for comparison purposes.

Parrington, Vernon Louis. *Main Currents in American Thought.* New York, 1930. Largely superseded but still interesting conception of Adams.

Roelofs, Gerrit. "Henry Adams: Pessimism and the Intelligent Use of Doom," *English Literary History* (Spring, 1950). Detailed analysis of Adams' intention and method in *the Education.*

Samuels, Ernest. *The Young Henry Adams.* Cambridge, Mass., 1948.

_____. *Henry Adams: The Middle Years.* Cambridge, Mass., 1958. A three-volume biography; makes extensive use of unpublished papers and relates Adams to nineteenth century social and intellectual worlds.

_____. *Henry Adams: The Major Phase.* Cambridge, Mass., 1964.

Speare, Morris. *The Political Novel: Its Development in England And America.* New York, 1924. Consideration of Adams as a representative of a literary tradition.

Spiller, Robert, et al. *Literary History of the United States*. New York, 1946. Balanced introduced to Adams as literary artist.

Stevenson, Elizabeth. *Henry Adams*. New York, 1955. Examination of the conflicts in Adams' life.

Winters, Yvor. *The Anatomy of Nonsense*. Norfolk, Conn., 1943. Analysis of the relationship of Adams and the Puritan tradition.

www.ingramcontent.com/pod-product-compliance
Lightning Source LLC
LaVergne TN
LVHW011732060526
838200LV00051B/3161